JUL 1 0 1998

D1551517

LONDON

THE WORLD 100 YEARS AGO

BERLIN

EGYPT

THE CITIES OF JAPAN

LONDON

MOSCOW

PARIS

PEKING

SOUTHERN ITALY

BURTON HOLMES

LONDON

FRED L. ISRAEL
General Editor

ARTHUR M. SCHLESINGER, JR.
Senior Consulting Editor

CHELSEA HOUSE PUBLISHERS
Philadelphia

CHELSEA HOUSE PUBLISHERS

EDITOR-IN-CHIEF Stephen Reginald
MANAGING EDITOR James D. Gallagher
PRODUCTION MANAGER Pamela Loos
ART DIRECTOR Sara Davis
PICTURE EDITOR Judy Hasday
SENIOR PRODUCTION EDITOR Lisa Chippendale
ASSOCIATE ART DIRECTOR Takeshi Takahashi
COVER DESIGN Dave Loose Design

First Printing

1 3 5 7 9 8 6 4 2

Library of Congress Cataloging-in-Publication Data

Holmes, Burton, b. 1870.
London/ Burton Holmes; Fred L. Israel, general editor; Arthur M. Schlesinger, jr., senior consulting editor.
    p. cm. —(The world 100 years ago)
A travelogue in text and photographs of London, 1897-1910. Includes bibliographical references and index.

ISBN 0-7910-4660-5 (hc). ISBN 0-7910-4661-3 (pb).

1. London (England)—History—1800-1950—Pictorial works. 2. London (England)—Description and travel. I. Israel, Fred L. II. Schlesinger, Arthur Meier, 1917- . III. Title. IV. Series: Holmes, Burton, b. 1870. World 100 years ago today.
DA684.H58   1997
914.2104'82—dc21   97-33419
                                             CIP

CONTENTS

———

THE GREAT GLOBE TROTTER

By Irving Wallace

One day in the year 1890, Miss Nellie Bly, of the *New York World,* came roaring into Brooklyn on a special train from San Francisco. In a successful effort to beat Phileas Fogg's fictional 80 days around the world, Miss Bly, traveling with two handbags and flannel underwear, had circled the globe in 72 days, 6 hours, and 11 minutes. Immortality awaited her.

Elsewhere that same year, another less-publicized globe-girdler made his start toward immortality. He was Mr. Burton Holmes, making his public debut with slides and anecdotes ("Through Europe With a Kodak") before the Chicago Camera Club. Mr. Holmes, while less spectacular than his feminine rival, was destined, for that very reason, soon to dethrone her as America's number-one traveler.

Today, Miss Bly and Mr. Holmes have one thing in common: In the mass mind they are legendary vagabonds relegated to the dim and dusty past of the Iron Horse and the paddle-wheel steamer. But if Miss Bly, who shuffled off this mortal coil in 1922, is now only a part of our folklore, there are millions to testify that

Mr. Burton Holmes, aged seventy-six, is still very much with us.

Remembering that Mr. Holmes was an active contemporary of Miss Bly's, that he was making a livelihood at traveling when William McKinley, John L. Sullivan, and Admiral Dewey ruled the United States, when Tony Pastor, Lily Langtry, and Lillian Russell ruled the amusement world, it is at once amazing and reassuring to pick up the daily newspapers of 1946 and find, sandwiched between advertisements of rash young men lecturing on "Inside Stalin" and "I Was Hitler's Dentist," calm announcements that tomorrow evening Mr. Burton Holmes has something more to say about "Beautiful Bali."

Burton Holmes, a brisk, immaculate, chunky man with gray Vandyke beard, erect bearing, precise speech ("folks are always mistaking me for Monty Woolley," he says, not unhappily), is one of the seven wonders of the entertainment world. As Everyman's tourist, Burton Holmes has crossed the Atlantic Ocean thirty times, the Pacific Ocean twenty times, and has gone completely around the world six times. He has spent fifty-five summers abroad, and recorded a half million feet of film of those summers. He was the first person to take motion picture cameras into Russia and Japan. He witnessed the regular decennial performance of the Passion Play at Oberammergau in 1890, and attended the first modern Olympics at Athens in 1896. He rode on the first Trans-Siberian train across Russia, and photographed the world's first airplane meet at Rheims.

As the fruit of these travels, Burton Holmes has delivered approximately 8,000 illustrated lectures that have grossed, according to an estimate by *Variety,* five million dollars in fifty-three winters. Because he does not like to be called a lecturer— "I'm a performer," he insists, "and I have performed on more legitimate stages than platforms"—he invented the word "travelogue" in London to describe his activity.

His travelogues, regarded as a fifth season of the year in most communities, have won him such popularity that he holds the record for playing in the longest one-man run in American show business. In the five and a half decades past, Burton Holmes has successively met the hectic competition of big-time vaudeville, stage, silent pictures, radio, and talking pictures, and he has survived them all.

At an age when most men have retired to slippered ease or are hounded by high blood pressure, Burton Holmes is more active and more popular than ever before. In the season just finished, which he started in San Francisco during September, 1945, and wound up in New York during April, 1946, Holmes appeared in 187 shows, a record number. He averaged six travelogues a week, spoke for two hours at each, and did 30 percent more box-office business than five years ago. Not once was a scheduled lecture postponed or canceled. In fact, he has missed only two in his life. In 1935, flying over the Dust Bowl, he suffered laryngitis and was forced to bypass two college dates. He has never canceled an appearance before a paid city audience. Seven years ago, when one of his elderly limbs was fractured in an automobile crack-up in Finland, there was a feeling that Burton Holmes might not make the rounds. When news of the accident was released, it was as if word had gone out that Santa Claus was about to cancel his winter schedule. But when the 1939 season dawned, Burton Holmes rolled on the stage in a wheelchair, and from his seat of pain (and for 129 consecutive appearances thereafter), he delivered his travel chat while 16-mm film shimmered on the screen beside him.

Today, there is little likelihood that anything, except utter extinction, could keep Holmes from his waiting audiences. Even now, between seasons, Holmes is in training for his next series— 150 illustrated lectures before groups in seventeen states.

Before World War II, accompanied by Margaret Oliver, his wife of thirty-two years, Holmes would spend his breathing spells on summery excursions through the Far East or Europe. While aides captured scenery on celluloid, Holmes wrote accompanying lecture material in his notebooks. Months later, he would communicate his findings to his cult, at a maximum price of $1.50 per seat. With the outbreak of war, Holmes changed his pattern. He curtailed travel outside the Americas. This year, except for one journey to Las Vegas, Nevada, where he personally photographed cowboy cutups and shapely starlets at the annual Helldorado festival, Holmes has been allowing his assistants to do all his traveling for him.

Recently, one crew, under cameraman Thayer Soule, who helped shoot the Battle of Tarawa for the Marines, brought Holmes a harvest of new film from Mexico. Another crew, after four months in Brazil last year, and two in its capital this year, returned to Holmes with magnificent movies. Meantime, other crews, under assignment from Holmes, are finishing films on Death Valley, the West Indies, and the Mississippi River.

In a cottage behind his sprawling Hollywood hilltop home, Holmes is busy, day and night, sorting the incoming negative, cutting and editing it, and rewriting lectures that will accompany the footage this winter. He is too busy to plan his next trip. Moreover, he doesn't feel that he should revisit Europe yet. "I wouldn't mind seeing it," he says, "but I don't think my public would be interested. My people want a good time, they want escape, they want sweetness and light, beauty and charm. There is too much rubble and misery over there now, and I'll let those picture magazines and Fox Movietone newsreels show all that. I'll wait until it's tourist time again."

When he travels, he thinks he will visit three of the four accessible places on earth that he has not yet seen. One is Tahiti, which he barely missed a dozen times, and the other two are Iran and Iraq. The remaining country that he has not seen, and has no wish to see, is primitive Afghanistan. Of all cities on earth, he would most like to revisit Kyoto, once capital of Japan. He still recalls that the first movies ever made inside Japan were ones he made in Kyoto, in 1899. The other cities he desires to revisit are

Venice and Rome. The only island for which he has any longing is Bali—"the one quaint spot on earth where you can really get away from it all."

In preparing future subjects, Holmes carefully studies the success of his past performances. Last season, his two most popular lectures in the East were "California" and "Adventures in Mexico." The former grossed $5,100 in two Chicago shows; the latter jammed the St. Louis Civic Auditorium with thirty-five hundred potential señores and señoritas. Holmes will use these subjects again, with revisions, next season, and add some brand-new Latin American and United States topics. He will sidestep anything relating to war. He feels, for example, that anything dealing with the once exotic Pacific islands might have a questionable reception—"people will still remember those white crosses they saw in newsreels of Guadalcanal and Iwo Jima."

Every season presents its own obstacles, and the next will challenge Holmes with a new audience of travel-sated and disillusioned ex-GI's. Many of these men, and their families, now know that a South Sea island paradise means mosquitoes and malaria and not Melville's Fayaway and Loti's Rarahu. They know Europe means mud and ruins and not romance. Nevertheless, Holmes is confident that he will win these people over.

"The veterans of World War II will come to my travelogues just as their fathers did. After the First World War, I gave illustrated lectures on the sights of France, and the ex-doughboys enjoyed them immensely. But I suppose there's no use comparing that war to this. The First World War was a minor dispute between gentlemen. In this one, the atrocities and miseries will be difficult to forget. I know I can't give my Beautiful Italy lecture next season to men who know Italy only as a pigsty, but you see, in my heart Italy is forever beautiful, and I see things in Italy they can't see, poor fellows. How could they? . . . Still, memory is frail, and one day these boys will forget and come to my lectures not to hoot but to relive the better moments and enjoy themselves."

While Burton Holmes prepares his forthcoming shows, his business manager, a slightly built dynamo named Walter Everest, works on next season's bookings. Everest contacts organizations interested in sponsoring a lecture series, arranges dates and prices, and often leases auditoriums on his own. Everest concentrates on cities where Holmes is known to be popular, Standing Room Only cities like New York, Boston, Philadelphia, Chicago, Los Angeles. On the other hand, he is cautious about the cities where Holmes has been unpopular in the past—Toledo, Cleveland, Indianapolis, Cincinnati. The one city Holmes now avoids entirely is Pomona, California, where, at a scheduled Saturday matinee, he found himself facing an almost empty house. The phenomenon of a good city or a poor city is inexplicable. In rare cases, there may be a reason for failure, and then Holmes will attempt to resolve it. When San Francisco was stone-deaf to Holmes, investigation showed that he had been competing with the annual opera season. Last year, he rented a theater the week before the opera began. He appeared eight times and made a handsome profit.

Once Holmes takes to the road for his regular season, he is a perpetual-motion machine. Leaving his wife behind, he barnstorms with his manager, Everest, and a projectionist, whirling to Western dates in his Cadillac, making long hops by plane, following the heavier Eastern circuit by train. Holmes likes to amaze younger men with his activities during a typical week. If he speaks in Detroit on a Tuesday night, he will lecture in Chicago on Wednesday evening, in Milwaukee on Thursday, be back in Chicago for Friday evening and a Saturday matinee session, then go on to Kansas City on Sunday, St. Louis on Monday, and play a return engagement in Detroit on Tuesday.

This relentless merry-go-round (with Saturday nights off to attend a newsreel "and see what's happening in the world") invigorates Holmes, but grinds his colleagues to a frazzle. One morning last season, after weeks of trains and travel, Walter

Everest was awakened by a porter at six. He rose groggily, sat swaying on the edge of his berth trying to put on his shoes. He had the look of a man who had pushed through the Matto Grosso on foot. He glanced up sleepily, and there, across the aisle, was Holmes, fully dressed, looking natty and refreshed. Holmes smiled sympathetically. "I know, Walter," he said, "this life is tiring. One day both of us ought to climb on some train and get away from it all."

In his years on the road, Holmes has come to know his audience thoroughly. He is firm in the belief that it is composed mostly of traveled persons who wish to savor the glamorous sights of the world again. Through Burton, they relive their own tours. Of the others, some regard a Holmes performance as a preview. They expect to travel; they want to know the choice sights for their future three-month jaunt to Ecuador. Some few, who consider themselves travel authorities, come to a Holmes lecture to point out gleefully the good things that he missed. "It makes them happy," Holmes says cheerfully. Tomorrow's audience, for the most, will be the same as the one that heard the Master exactly a year before. Generations of audiences inherit Holmes, one from the other.

An average Holmes lecture combines the atmosphere of a revival meeting and a family get-together at which home movies are shown. A typical Holmes travelogue begins in a brightly lit auditorium, at precisely three minutes after eight-thirty. The three minutes is to allow for latecomers. Holmes, attired in formal evening clothes, strides from the wings to center stage. People applaud; some cheer. Everyone seems to know him and to know exactly what to expect. Holmes smiles broadly. He is compact, proper, handsome. His goatee dominates the scene. He has worn it every season, with the exception of one in 1895 (when, beardless, he somewhat resembled Paget's Sherlock Holmes). Now, he speaks crisply. He announces that this is the third lecture of his fifty-fourth season. He announces his subject—"Adventures in Mexico."

He walks to one side of the stage, where a microphone is standing. The lights are dimmed. The auditorium becomes dark. Beyond the fifth row, Holmes cannot be seen. The all-color 16-mm film is projected on the screen. The film opens, minus title and credits, with a shot through the windshield of an automobile speeding down the Pan-American Highway to Monterrey. Holmes himself is the sound track. His speech, with just the hint of a theatrical accent, is intimate, as if he were talking in a living room. He punctuates descriptive passages with little formal jokes. When flowers and orange trees of Mexico are on the screen, he says, "We have movies and talkies, but now we should have smellies and tasties"—and he chuckles.

The film that he verbally captions is a dazzling, uncritical montage of Things Mexican. There is a señora selling tortillas, and close-ups of how tortillas are made. There is a bullfight, but not the kill. There is snow-capped Popocatepetl, now for sale at the bargain price of fifteen million dollars. There are the pyramids outside Mexico City, older than those of Egypt, built by the ancient Toltecs who went to war with wooden swords so that they would not kill their enemies.

Holmes's movies and lectures last two hours, with one intermission. The emphasis is on description, information, and oddity. Two potential ingredients are studiously omitted. One is adventure, the other politics. Holmes is never spectacular. "I want nothing dangerous. I don't care to emulate the explorers, to risk my neck, to be the only one or the first one there. Let others tackle the Himalayas, the Amazon, the North Pole, let them break the trails for me. I'm just a Cook's tourist, a little ahead of the crowd, but not too far ahead." Some years ago, Holmes did think that he was an explorer, and became very excited about it, he now admits sheepishly. This occurred in a trackless sector of Northern Rhodesia. Holmes felt that he had discovered a site never before seen by an outsider. Grandly, he planted the flag of the Explorers

Club, carefully he set up his camera, and then, as he prepared to shoot, his glance fell upon an object several feet away—an empty Kodak carton. Quietly, he repacked and stole away—and has stayed firmly on the beaten paths ever since.

As to politics, it never taints his lectures. He insists neither he nor his audiences are interested. "When you discuss politics," he says, "you are sure to offend." Even after his third trip to Russia, he refused to discuss politics. "I am a traveler," he explained at that time, "and not a student of political and economic questions. To me, Communism is merely one of the sights I went to see."

However, friends know that Holmes has his pet panacea for the ills of the world. He is violent about the gold standard, insisting that it alone can make all the world prosperous. Occasionally, when the mood is on him, and against his better judgment, he will inject propaganda in favor of the gold standard into an otherwise timid travelogue.

When he is feeling mellow, Holmes will confess that once in the past he permitted politics to intrude upon his sterile chitchat. It was two decades ago, when he jousted with Prohibition. While not a dedicated drinking man, Holmes has been on a friendly basis with firewater since the age of sixteen. In the ensuing years, he has regularly, every dusk before dinner, mixed himself one or two highballs. Only once did he try more than two, and the results were disastrous. "Any man who drinks three will drink three hundred," he now says righteously. Holmes felt that Prohibition was an insult to civilized living. As a consequence of this belief, his audiences during the days of the Eighteenth Amendment were often startled to hear Holmes extol the virtues of open drinking, in the middle of a placid discourse on Oberammergau or Lapland. "Sometimes an indignant female would return her tickets to the rest of my series," he says, "but there were others, more intelligent, to take her place."

This independent attitude in Holmes was solely the product of his personal success. Born in January, 1870, of a financially secure, completely cosmopolitan Chicago family, he was able to be independent from his earliest days. His father, an employee in the Third National Bank, distinguished himself largely by lending George Pullman enough cash to transform his old day coaches into the first Pullman Palace Sleeping Cars, and by refusing a half interest in the business in exchange for his help. Even to this day, it makes Burton Holmes dizzy to think of the money he might have saved in charges for Pullman berths.

Holmes's interest in show business began at the age of nine when his grandmother, Ann W. Burton, took him to hear John L. Stoddard lecture on the Passion Play at Oberammergau. Young Holmes was never the same again. After brief visits to faraway Florida and California, he quit school and accompanied his grandmother on his first trip abroad. He was sixteen and wide-eyed. His grandmother, who had traveled with her wine-salesman husband to France and Egypt and down the Volga in the sixties, was the perfect guide. But this journey through Europe was eclipsed, four years later, by a more important pilgrimage with his grandmother to Germany. The first day at his hotel in Munich, Holmes saw John L. Stoddard pass through the lobby reading a Baedeker. He was petrified. It was as if he had seen his Maker. Even now, over a half century later, when Holmes speaks about Stoddard, his voice carries a tinge of awe. For eighteen years of the later nineteenth century, Stoddard, with black-and-white slides and magnificent oratory, dominated the travel-lecture field. To audiences, young and old, he was the most romantic figure in America. Later, at Oberammergau, Holmes sat next to Stoddard through the fifteen acts of the Passion Play and they became friends.

When Holmes returned to the States, some months after Nellie Bly had made her own triumphal return to Brooklyn, he showed rare Kodak negatives of his travels to fellow members of the Chicago Camera Club. The members were impressed, and one suggested that these be mounted as slides and shown to the general public. "To take the edge off the silence, to keep the show moving," says Holmes, "I wrote an account of my journey and read it, as the stereopticon man changed slides." The show, which grossed the club $350, was Holmes's initial travelogue. However, he dates the beginning of his professional career from three years later, when he appeared under his own auspices with hand-colored slides.

After the Camera Club debut, Holmes did not go immediately into the travelogue field. He was not yet ready to appreciate its possibilities. Instead, he attempted to sell real estate, and failed. Then he worked for eight dollars a week as a photo supply clerk. In 1902, aching with wanderlust, he bullied his family into staking him to a five-month tour of Japan. On the boat he was thrilled to find John L. Stoddard, also bound for Japan. They became closer friends, even though they saw Nippon through different eyes. "The older man found Japan queer, quaint, comfortless, and almost repellent," Stoddard's son wrote years later. "To the younger man it was a fairyland." Stoddard invited Holmes to continue on around the world with him, but Holmes loved Japan and decided to remain.

When Holmes returned to Chicago, the World's Columbian Exposition of 1893 was in full swing. He spent months at the Jackson Park grounds, under Edison's new electric lights, listening to Lillian Russell sing, Susan B. Anthony speak, and watching Sandow perform feats of strength. With rising excitement, he observed Jim Brady eating, Anthony Comstock snorting at Little Egypt's hootchy-kootchy, and Alexander Dowie announcing himself as the Prophet Elijah III.

In the midst of this excitement came the depression of that year. Holmes's father suffered. "He hit the wheat pit at the wrong time, and I had to go out on my own," says Holmes. "The photo supply house offered me fifteen dollars a week to return. But I didn't want to work. The trip to Japan, the Oriental exhibits of the Exposition, were still on my mind. I thought of

Stoddard. I thought of the slides I'd had hand-colored in Tokyo. That was it, and it wasn't work. So I hired a hall and became a travel lecturer."

Copying society addresses from his mother's visiting list, and additional addresses from *The Blue Book,* Holmes mailed two thousand invitations in the form of Japanese poem-cards. Recipients were invited to two illustrated lectures, at $1.50 each, on "Japan—the Country and the Cities." Both performances were sellouts. Holmes grossed $700.

For four years Holmes continued his fight to win a steady following, but with only erratic success. Then, in 1897, when he stood at the brink of defeat, two events occurred to change his life. First, John L. Stoddard retired from the travel-lecture field and threw the platforms of the nation open to a successor. Second, Holmes supplemented colored slides with a new method of illustrating his talks. As his circular announced, "There will be presented for the first time in connection with a course of travel lectures a series of pictures to which a modern miracle has added the illusion of life itself—the reproduction of recorded motion."

Armed with his jumpy movies—scenes of the Omaha fire department, a police parade in Chicago, Italians eating spaghetti, each reel running twenty-five seconds, with a four-minute wait between reels—Burton Holmes invaded the Stoddard strongholds in the East. Stoddard came to hear him and observe the newfangled movies. Like Marshal Foch who regarded the airplane as "an impractical toy," Stoddard saw no future in the motion picture. Nevertheless, he gave young Holmes a hand by insisting that Augustin Daly lease his Manhattan theater to the newcomer. This done, Stoddard retired to the Austrian Tyrol, and Holmes went on to absorb Stoddard's audiences in Boston and Philadelphia and to win new followers of his own throughout the nation.

His success assured, Holmes began to gather material with a vigor that was to make him one of history's most indefatigable travelers. In 1900, at the Paris Exposition, sitting in a restaurant built like a Russian train, drinking vodka while a colored panorama of Siberia rolled past his window, he succumbed to this unique advertising of the new Trans-Siberian railway and bought a ticket. The trip in 1901 was a nightmare. After ten days on the Trans-Siberian train, which banged along at eleven miles an hour, Holmes was dumped into a construction train for five days, and then spent twenty-seven days on steamers going down the Amur River. It took him forty-two and a half days to travel from Moscow to Vladivostok.

But during that tour, he had one great moment. He saw Count Leo Tolstoi at Yasnaya Polyana, the author's country estate near Tula. At a dinner in Moscow, Holmes met Albert J. Beveridge, the handsome senator from Indiana. Beveridge had a letter of introduction to Tolstoi and invited Holmes and his enormous 60-mm movie camera to come along. Arriving in a four-horse landau, the Americans were surprised to find Tolstoi's house dilapidated. Then, they were kept waiting two hours. At last, the seventy-three-year-old, white-bearded Tolstoi, nine years away from his lonely death in a railway depot, appeared. He was attired in a mujik costume. He invited his visitors to breakfast, then conversed in fluent English. "He had only a slight accent, and he spoke with the cadence of Sir Henry Irving," Holmes recalls.

Of the entire morning's conversation, Holmes remembers clearly only one remark. That was when Tolstoi harangued, "There should be no law. No man should have the right to judge or condemn another. Absolute freedom of the individual is the only thing that can redeem the world. Christ was a great teacher, nothing more!" As Tolstoi continued to speak, Holmes quietly set up his movie camera. Tolstoi had never seen one before. He posed stiffly, as for a daguerreotype. When he thought that it was over, and resumed his talking, Holmes began actual shooting. This priceless film never reached the screen. Senator Beveridge was then a presidential possibility. His managers feared that this film of Beveridge with a Russian radical might be used by his opponents. The film was taken from Holmes and destroyed. Later, when he was not even nominated for the presidency, Beveridge wrote an apology to Holmes, "for this destruction of so valuable a living record of the grand old Russian."

In 1934, at a cost of ten dollars a day, Holmes spent twenty-one days in modern Soviet Russia. He loved the ballet, the omelets, the Russian rule against tipping, and the lack of holdups. He went twice to see the embalmed Lenin, fascinated by the sight of "his head resting on a red pillow like that of a tired man asleep."

Although Holmes's name had already appeared on eighteen travel volumes, this last Russian trip inspired him to write his first and only original book. The earlier eighteen volumes, all heavily illustrated, were offered as a set, of which over forty thousand were sold. However, they were not "written," but were actually a collection of lectures delivered orally by Holmes. The one book that he wrote as a book, *The Traveler's Russia,* published in 1934 by G.P. Putnam's Sons, was a failure. Holmes has bought the remainders and passes them out to guests with a variety of inscriptions. In a serious mood he will inscribe, "To travel is to possess the world." In a frivolous mood, he will write "With love from Tovarich Burtonovich Holmeski."

In the five decades past, Holmes has kept himself occupied with a wide variety of pleasures, such as attending Queen Victoria's Golden Jubilee in London, chatting with Admiral Dewey in Hong Kong, driving the first automobile seen in Denmark, and photographing a mighty eruption of Vesuvius.

In 1918, wearing a war correspondent's uniform, he shot army scenes on the Western Front and his films surpassed those of the poorly organized newsreel cameramen. In 1923, flying for the first time, he had his most dangerous experience, when his plane almost crashed between Toulouse and Rabat. Later, in

Berlin, he found his dollar worth ten million marks, and in Africa he interviewed Emperor Haile Selassie in French, and, closer to home, he flew 20,000 miles over Central and South America.

Burton Holmes enjoys company on his trips. By coincidence, they are often celebrities. Holmes traveled through Austria with Maria Jeritza, through Greece with E.F. Benson, through the Philippines with Dr. Victor Heiser. He covered World War I with Harry Franck, wandered about Japan with Lafcadio Hearn's son, crossed Ethiopia with the Duke of Gloucester. He saw Hollywood with Mary Pickford, Red Square with Alma Gluck, and the Andes with John McCutcheon.

Of the hundreds of travelogues that Holmes has delivered, the most popular was "The Panama Canal." He offered this in 1912, when the "big ditch" was under construction, and news-hungry citizens flocked to hear him. Among less timely subjects, his most popular was the standard masterpiece on Oberammergau, followed closely by his illustrated lectures on the "Frivolities of Paris," the "Canals of Venice," the "Countryside of England" and, more currently, "Adventures in Mexico." Burton Holmes admits that his greatest failure was an elaborate travelogue on Siam, even though it seemed to have everything except Anna and the King thereof. Other failures included travelogues on India, Burma, Ethiopia, and—curiously—exotic Bali. The only two domestic subjects to fizzle were "Down in Dixie" in 1915 and "The Century of Progress Exposition" in 1932.

All in all, the success of Holmes's subjects has been so consistently high that he has never suffered seriously from competition. One rival died, another retired eight years ago. "I'm the lone survivor of the magic-lantern boys," says Holmes. Of the younger crowd, Holmes thought that Richard Halliburton might become his successor. "He deserved to carry the banner," says Holmes. "He was good-looking, with a fine classical background, intelligent, interesting, and he really did those darn-fool stunts." Halliburton, who had climbed the Matterhorn, swum the Hellespont, followed the Cortés train through Mexico, lectured with slides. "I told him to throw away the slides," says Holmes. "He was better without them, his speech was so colorful." When Halliburton died attempting to sail a Chinese junk across the Pacific, Holmes decided to present an illustrated lecture on "The Romantic Adventures of Richard Halliburton." He used his own movies but, in the accompanying talk, Halliburton's written text. "It was a crashing failure," sighs Holmes. "His millions of fans did not want to hear me, and my fans did not want to know about him."

For a while, Hollywood appeared to be the travelogue's greatest threat. Holmes defeated this menace by marriage with the studios. He signed a contract with Paramount, made fifty-two travel shorts each year, between 1915 and 1921. Then, with the advent of talking pictures, Holmes joined Metro-Goldwyn-Mayer and made a series of travelogues, released in English, French, Italian, Spanish. In 1933, he made his debut in radio, and in 1944 made his first appearance on television.

Today, safe in the knowledge that he is an institution, Holmes spends more and more time in his rambling, plantation-style, wooden home, called "Topside," located on a hill a mile above crowded Hollywood Boulevard. This dozen-roomed brown house, once a riding club for silent day film stars, and owned for six years by Francis X. Bushman (who gave it Hollywood's first swimming pool, where Holmes now permits neighborhood children to splash), was purchased by Holmes in 1930. "I had that M-G-M contract," he says, "and it earned me a couple of hundred thousand dollars. Well, everyone with a studio contract immediately gets himself a big car, a big house, and a small blonde. I acquired the car, the house, but kept the blonde a mental acquisition." For years, Holmes also owned a Manhattan duplex decorated with costly Japanese and Buddhist treasures, which he called "Nirvana." Before Pearl Harbor, Holmes sold the duplex, with its two-million-dollar collection of furnishings, to Robert Ripley, the cartoonist and oddity hunter.

Now, in his rare moments of leisure, Holmes likes to sit on the veranda of his Hollywood home and chat with his wife. Before he met her, he had been involved in one public romance. Gossips, everywhere, insisted that he might marry the fabulous Elsie de Wolfe, actress, millionaire decorator, friend of Oscar Wilde and Sarah Bernhardt, who later became Lady Mendl. Once, in Denver, Holmes recalls, a reporter asked him if he was engaged to Elsie de Wolfe. Holmes replied, curtly, No. That afternoon a banner headline proclaimed: BURTON HOLMES REFUSES TO MARRY ELSIE DE WOLFE!

Shortly afterward, during a photographic excursion, Holmes met Margaret Oliver who, suffering from deafness, had taken up still photography as an avocation. In 1914, following a moonlight proposal on a steamer's deck, he married Miss Oliver in New York City's St. Stephen's Episcopal Church, and took her to prosaic Atlantic City for the first few days of their honeymoon, then immediately embarked on a long trip abroad.

When his wife is out shopping, Holmes will stroll about his estate, study his fifty-four towering palm trees, return to the veranda for a highball, thumb through the *National Geographic,* play with his cats, or pick up a language textbook. He is on speaking terms with eight languages, including some of the Scandinavian, and is eager to learn more. He never reads travel books. "As Pierre Loti once remarked, 'I don't read. It might ruin my style,'" he explains.

He likes visitors, and he will startle them with allusions to his earlier contemporaries. "This lawn part reminds me of the one at which I met Emperor Meiji," he will say. Meiji, grandfather of Hirohito, opened Japan to Commodore Perry. When visitors ask for his travel advice, Holmes invariably tells them to see the Americas first. "Why go to Mont St. Michel?" he asks. "Have you seen Monticello?"

But when alone with his wife and co-workers on the veranda,

and the pressure of the new season is weeks away, he will loosen his blue dressing gown, inhale, then stare reflectively out over the sun-bathed city below.

"You know, this is the best," he will say softly, "looking down on this Los Angeles. It is heaven. I could sit here the rest of my life." Then, suddenly, he will add, "There is so much else to see and do. If only I could have another threescore years upon this planet. If only I could know the good earth better than I do."

———

Note: Irving Wallace (1916-1990) wrote this article on the occasion of Burton Holmes's 77th birthday. It was originally printed in *The Saturday Evening Post* May 10, 1947. Holmes retired the following year from presenting his travelogues in person. He died in 1958 at age 88. His autobiography, *The World is Mine,* was published in 1953.

Reprinted by permission of Mrs. Sylvia Wallace.

BURTON HOLMES

By Arthur M. Schlesinger, jr.

B urton Holmes!—forgotten today, but such a familiar name in America in the first half of the 20th century, a name then almost synonymous with dreams of foreign travel. In the era before television brought the big world into the households of America, it was Burton Holmes who brought the world to millions of Americans in crowded lecture halls, and did so indefatigably for 60 years. I still remember going with my mother in the 1920s to Symphony Hall in Boston, watching the brisk, compact man with a Vandyke beard show his films of Venice or Bali or Kyoto and describe foreign lands in engaging and affectionate commentary.

Burton Holmes invented the word "travelogue" in 1904. He embodied it for the rest of his life. He was born in Chicago in 1870 and made his first trip abroad at the age of 16. Taking a camera along on his second trip, he mounted his black-and-white negatives on slides and showed them to friends in the Chicago Camera Club. "To keep the show moving," he said later, "I wrote an account of my journey and read it, as the stereopticon man changed slides." He had discovered his métier. Soon he had his slides hand-colored and was in business as a professional lecturer. In time, as technology developed, slides gave way to moving pictures.

Holmes was a tireless traveler, forever ebullient and optimistic, uninterested in politics and poverty and the darker side of life, in love with beautiful scenery, historic monuments, picturesque customs, and challenging trips. He was there at the Athens Olympics in 1896, at the opening of the Trans-Siberian railway, at the Passion Play in Oberammergau. His popular lectures had such titles as "The Magic of Mexico," "The Canals of Venice," "The Glories and Frivolities of Paris." His illustrated travel books enthralled thousands of American families. He also filmed a series of travelogues—silent pictures for Paramount, talkies for Metro-Goldwyn-Mayer.

He wanted his fellow countrymen to rejoice in the wonders of the great globe. "I'm a Cook's tourist," he said, referring to the famous tours conducted by Thomas Cook and Sons, "reporting how pleasant it is in such and such a place." He knew that the world was less than perfect, but he thought the worst sufficiently documented, and his mission, as he saw it, was to bring people the best. Reflecting at the end of the Second World War on the mood of returning veterans, he said, "The atrocities and miseries will be difficult to forget. I know I can't give my Beautiful Italy lecture next session to men who know Italy only as a pigsty . . . One day these boys will forget and come to my lectures not to hoot but to relive the better moments and enjoy themselves."

When he retired in 1951, Burton Holmes had delivered over 8,000 lectures. By the time he died in 1958, television had taken over the job he had discharged so ardently for more than half a century. He taught generations of Americans about the great world beyond the seas. His books are still readable today and show new generations how their grandparents learned about a world that has since passed away but remains a fragrant memory.

THE WORLD 100 YEARS AGO

By Dr. Fred Israel

The generation that lived 100 years ago was the first to leave behind a comprehensive visual record. It was the camera that made this possible. The great photographers of the 1860s and 1870s took their unwieldy equipment to once-unimaginable places—from the backstreets of London to the homesteads of the American frontier; from tribal Africa to the temples of Japan. They photographed almost the entire world.

Burton Holmes (1870-1958) ranks among the pioneers who popularized photojournalism. He had an insatiable curiosity. "There was for me the fascination of magic in photography," Holmes wrote. "The word Kodak had not yet been coined. You could not press the button and let someone else do the rest. You had to do it all yourself and know what you were doing." Holmes combined his love of photography with a passion for travel. It didn't really matter where—only that it be exciting.

"Shut your eyes, tight!" said Holmes. "Imagine the sands of the Sahara, the temples of Japan, the beach at Waikiki, the fjords of Norway, the vastness of Panama, the great gates of Peking." It was this type of visual imagination that made Burton Holmes America's best known travel lecturer. By his 75th birthday, he had crossed the Atlantic Ocean 30 times and the Pacific 20, and he had gone around the world on six occasions. Variety magazine estimated that in his five-decade career, Holmes had delivered more than 8,000 lectures describing almost every corner of the earth.

Burton Holmes was born in Chicago on January 8, 1870. His privileged background contributed to his lifelong fascination with travel. When he was 16, his maternal grandmother took him on a three-month European trip, about which he later wrote:

> I still recall our first meal ashore, the delicious English sole served at the Adelphi Hotel [Liverpool] . . . Edinburgh thrilled me, but Paris! I would gladly have travelled third class or on a bike or on foot. Paris at last! I knew my Paris in advance. Had I not studied the maps and plans? I knew I could find my way to Notre Dame and to the Invalides without asking anyone which way to go. (The Eiffel Tower had not yet been built.) From a bus-top, I surveyed the boulevards—recognizing all the famous sights. Then for a panoramic survey of the city, I climbed the towers of Notre Dame, then the Tour St. Jacques, the Bastille Column, and finally the Arc De Triomphe, all in one long day. That evening, I was in Montmartre, where as yet there stood no great domed church of the Sacre Coeur. But at the base of the famous hill were the red windmill wings of the Moulin Rouge revolving in all their majesty. My French—school French—was pretty bad but it sufficed. Paris was the springtime of my life!

Holmes never lost his passion for travel nor his passion for capturing his observations on film. He has left us with a unique and remarkable record that helps us to visualize the world many decades ago.

Lecturing became Holmes's profession. In 1892-93 he toured Japan. He discovered that "it was my native land in some previous incarnation—and the most beautiful land I have known." Holmes had the idea of giving an illustrated lecture about Japan to an affluent Chicago audience:

> I had brought home a large number of Japanese cards such as
> are used in Japan for sending poems or New Year's greetings.
> They were about two inches by fourteen inches long. I had the
> idea that they would, by their odd shape, attract instant notice.
> So I had envelopes made for them, employing a Japanese artist
> to make a design.

Holmes sent about 2,000 invitations to the socially prominent
whose addresses he took from the *Blue Book*. He "invited" them
to two illustrated lectures at $1.50 each on "Japan—the Country
and the Cities." ($1.50 was a high sum for the 1890s considering
that the average worker earned about $1 per day.) Both perfor-
mances sold out.

Burton Holmes's "Travelogues" (he began using the term in
1904) rapidly became part of American upper class societal life.
Holmes engaged the best theater or concert hall for a week at a
time. His appearance was an annual event at Carnegie Hall in
New York, Symphony Hall in Boston, and Orchestra Hall in
Chicago. His uncanny instinct for exciting programs invariably
received rave reviews. Once he explained how he selected his
photographic subjects:

> If I am walking through Brussels and see a dog cart or some
> other unimportant thing that is interesting enough for me to
> watch it, I am totally certain others would be interested in seeing
> a photograph of it.

A conservative man, Holmes avoided political upheavals,
economic exploitation, and social conflicts in his travelogues.
"When you discuss politics," he said, "you are sure to offend."
Holmes focused on people, places, and customs. He offered his
audience a world which was unfailingly tranquil and beautiful.

In 1897, Holmes introduced motion picture segments into his
programs. ("Neapolitans Eating Spaghetti" was his first film
clip.) His engaging personality contributed to his success. His

crisp narrative was delivered in a pleasant and cultured tone. He always wore formal dress with striped pants before an audience. Holmes took pride in creating an atmosphere so that his listeners could imagine the "Magic of Mexico" or the "Frivolities of Paris." "My first ambition was to be a magician," he said. "And, I never departed from creating illusions. I have tried to create the illusion that we are going on a journey. By projecting the views, I tried to create the illusion we are looking through 'the window of travel' upon shifting scenes." Holmes's travelogues were immensely successful financially—and Holmes became one of history's most indefatigable travelers.

Holmes's lectures took place during the winter months between the 1890s and his retirement in the early 1950s. In between, he traveled—he crossed Morocco on horseback from oasis to oasis (1894); he was in the Philippines during the 1899 insurrection; in 1901, he traversed the Russian Empire, going from Moscow to Vladivostok in 43 days. He visited Yellowstone National Park (1896) before it had been fully mapped. He was always on the move, traveling to: Venice (1896); London (1897); Hawaii (1898); The Philippines (1899); Paris (1900); Russia, China, and Korea (1901-02); Madeira, Lisbon, Denmark, and Sweden (1902); Arizona, California, and Alaska (1903); Switzerland (1904); Russia and Japan (1905); Italy, Greece, Egypt, and Hong Kong (1906); Paris, Vienna, and Germany (1907); Japan (1908); Norway (1909); Germany and Austria (1910); Brazil, Argentina, and Peru (1911); Havana and Panama (1912); India and Burma (1913); the British Isles (1914); San Francisco (1915); Canada (1916); Australia and New Zealand (1917); Belgium and Germany (1919); Turkey and the Near East (1920); England (1921); China (1922); North Africa (1923); Italy (1924); Ceylon (1925); Holland (1926); France (1927); Spain (1928); London (1929); Ethiopia (1930); California (1931); Java (1932); Chicago (1933); the Soviet Union (1934); Normandy and Brittany (1935); South America (1936); South Africa (1937); Germany (1938).

Holmes's black and white photographs have extraordinary clarity. His sharp eye for the unusual ranks him as a truly out-standing photographer and chronicler of the world.

Holmes's lectures on the Panama Canal were his most popu-lar—cities added extra sessions. For Holmes though, his favorite presentation was always Paris—"no city charms and fascinates us like the city by the Seine." He found Athens in the morning to be the most beautiful scene in the world—"with its pearl lights and purple-blue shadows and the Acropolis rising in mystic grandeur." Above all though, Japan remained his favorite land—"one can peel away layer after layer of the serene contentment which we mistake for expressionlessness and find new beauties and surprises beneath each." And Kyoto, once the capital, was the place he wanted most to revisit—and revisit. Holmes never completed a travelogue of New York City—"I am saving the biggest thing in the world for the last." At the time of his death in 1958 at age 88, Holmes had visited most of the world. He repeat-edly told interviewers that he had lived an exciting and fulfilling life because he had accomplished his goal—to travel.

In a time before television, Burton Holmes was for many peo-ple "The Travelogue Man." He brought the glamour and excite-ment of foreign lands to Americans unable to go themselves. His successful career spanned the years from the Spanish-American War in 1898 to the Cold War of the 1950s—a period when Amer-icans were increasingly curious about distant places and peoples. During this time period, travel was confined to a comparative handful of the privileged. Holmes published travelogues explaining foreign cultures and customs to the masses.

In this series of splendid travel accounts, Holmes unfolds before our eyes the beauties of foreign lands as they appeared almost a century ago. These volumes contain hundreds of pho-tographs taken by Holmes. Through his narratives and illustra-tions we are transported in spirit to the most interesting countries and cities of the world.

LONDON

Burton Holmes's description of London, 1897-1910, is unique. I know of no other essay that combines a physical account of the city with a vivid description of how the people lived, from the aristocracy to the working-class poor. His stunning photographs visually convey the diverse economic and social conditions that existed in this bustling metropolis 100 years ago.

Holmes photographed the East End hovels, the wealthy West End mansions, the fish markets of Petticoat Lane, and the patrician buildings of Park Lane, whose address "upon a calling card is almost to transform that card into a social passport." He wrote about the cultural life of the privileged and of the public bathhouses of the poor. He described the fine hotels and the depressing tenements, the museums with their glorious holdings, and the shop-girl on a penny bus.

We learn from both the text and photographs how people lived, what they wore, how they celebrated holidays; we learn about the food markets and the new electrified Underground—a rail system which cleared "the smoke and gasses that for so many years threatened every passenger with asphyxiation." We learn about London's major class divisions, such as the Cockneys: "No Londoner will admit that a Cockney is a typical Londoner, yet all the world regards London as a community of Cockneys," Holmes explains. He describes the Coster peddlers, the open spaces "reserved as playgrounds for the London poor." He includes a photograph of a dog cemetary at Victoria Gate where the wealthy buried their family pets. Holmes's sharp eye also noted the American Quick Stand Lunch in the Strand where visiting New Yorkers gulped what to a Londoner is the deadliest of all American mixed drinks—ice water!

Holmes had a delightful sense of humor about himself and of

what he observed. He had tremendous knowledge and yet he retained a sort of innocence about other cultures. It is a wonderful experience to follow him through London; to explore with him the ruins of a Roman bath in a narrow street near the Strand. "How many of us even suspect that there is a Roman bath in London?" he asks his readers.

We join Holmes at every turn in this wonderful old city. He listens in amazement at Hyde Park Corner to the most outspoken "abuse of the government" which draws not a murmur of protest from the police. He notes with delight that one banner of the Amalgamated Society of Tailors was a representation of Adam and Eve in the Garden of Eden, "reminding us that man owes a great deal to his tailors." He opines about Westminster Abbey, where English kings and queens are crowned at a place filled with monuments in bad taste—bad plays, Holmes asserts, "will perish of their own demerits, but marble monuments, however atrocious, endure for generations."

What follows in these pages is a delightful travelogue of one of the great cities of the world, London. We see through Holmes's eyes, both in text and photographs, the city's people, and their traditions and customs.

FLEET STREET AND LUDGATE HILL

London

LONDON is the most important place on earth. It is not only the most populous, it is the greatest of great cities. No other city is the center of so many world-wide interests. Toward no other city do so many human beings look for inspiration, for commands, and for reward.

To the American, London means more than any other foreign city; we are related to its life: it is the Mother City, the *Metropolis*, not of England only, but of the entire English-speaking world.

Not to know London is to lack a standard by which to measure the merits or demerits of our great cities in America. Not to

know London is to be unable to recognize the shortcomings of our
newer cities — or to appreciate their magnificent achievements.

London is splendidly unbeautiful; its architecture, for the
most part, grandly ungraceful; its walls covered with a cleanly
grime.

London is leisurely animated; it roars in a gentle monotone,

THE THAMES

that to American ears, hardened to the clattering thunder of our
streets, seems almost quietude or silence.

In London dwells a population of over seven millions. The
citizens of London outnumber the sum total of the subjects of three
important European kingdoms: add all the Norwegians in Norway
and all the Danes in Denmark to all the Greeks in Greece, and you
will not have quite enough people to fill the places of the living
Londoners to-day. Among these living Londoners we find thousands of the most miserable and most debased of humankind,
and other thousands, representing the very flower — the per-
fected product — of centuries of Christian civilization.

The traveler's first grandiose glimpse of the World's Metropolis

SOMERSET HOUSE

is usually from the window of his "carriage" as the
arriving train rolls over the railway bridge to Charing
Cross. He sees the Thames, spanned by the many arches
of one of the world's finest bridges, the name of which
commemorates the victory of Waterloo. He sees beyond
it, to the left, the noble front of Somerset House, while
farther on rise the various buildings of the Temple;
but dominating all is the high-soaring dome, the most
conspicuous thing in London, the dome of St. Paul's
Cathedral.

Nearer, on the water's edge, stands the oldest object
in all London — the Egyptian obelisk, called "Cleo-
patra's Needle." But it is of an age anterior to
that of the Enchantress of the Nile; it was set
up at Heliopolis in Egypt by the Pharaoh,
Thotmes III, to commemorate one of his
many jubilees, more than thirty-three centuries ago. Two thousand years ago it
was brought to Alexandria by order of a
Roman Emperor, only to lie neglected in
the seaside sands beside its com-
panion shaft, which stands to-day in

THE OLDEST OBJECT IN LONDON

Central Park, New York. In 1820, Mohammed Ali, then master of Egypt, offered it to England.

Then, after England had hesitated nearly threescore years about picking up this dull old needle, an Englishman of public spirit spent fifty thousand dollars in bringing it hither from the land of the Sphinx and erecting it here on the Thames Embankment in 1878. It has outlived all the great cities, all the empires of antiquity. This obelisk has seen the ancient empires of Egypt, Greece, and Rome, and the modern empire of Napoleon rise, totter, and fall; and though the British Empire is standing firm, we feel a threatening prophecy in the lines that Tennyson put into the mouth of this thing of stone; he makes the obelisk exclaim, as if in warning to the pride of Britain:

"I have seen four great empires disappear —
I *was*, when London was not —
I am here!"

GUARDING THE OBELISK

FROM THE FIRE MONUMENT

But surely, London itself can never disappear; it is too big, too real, ever to pass away. This London, with its seven thousand miles of streets, is no mere creation of to-day. London has had a continuous existence for about two thousand years.

Just when the first savage Britons settled on this site has never been determined. The name, however, has been fairly well accounted for.

THE POOL OF LONDON

The Romans
called the place
Londinium, mak-
ing this name out
of the ancient Brit-
ish words, "Lin,"
which meant a
pool, and "Dun,"
which meant a
place of strength,
or a hill-fort.
Thus the name
means something
like

LONDON BRIDGE

"The Pool of the Strong Place on the Hill." That Pool of London still exists; it is the world-famous anchorage for sea-going ships in the Thames just below London Bridge. But it has lost much of its old-time animation since the creation of the vast London docks where the larger part of London's shipping now finds accommodation.

THE FIRE MONUMENT

As for the other syllable of London's name, the "Dun" or "Strong Place," was undoubtedly on the hill called Ludgate Hill, on which St. Paul's Cathedral stands to-day. The name Ludgate is said to come from old King Ludd, who ruled there just before the Romans came. London was at that time a hamlet

THE TOWER BRIDGE

of crude huts, surrounded by a forest and a marsh. How strange that so many great cities should have risen from marshes. St. Petersburg was built upon a marsh; Chicago stands on soggy soil; parts of Paris cover the old "*Marais*," and even to-day underground streams flow through a hidden marsh beneath this world of brick and stone that we call "London," and join the Thames not far from London Bridge.

A splendid point of vantage whence to look down on London Bridge is the top of the Fire Monument, raised to commemorate the conflagration of 1666, which burned up nearly ninety churches, nearly fourteen thousand houses, fifty-five million dollars' worth of property, and all the dormant germs of the plague; for since that fortunate fire London has been free from that old curse of medieval cities. The London Bridge of to-day in no way resembles its historic predecessor, which, like the Ponte Vecchio in Florence, was incrusted with shops and houses all the way from

THE TOWER OF LONDON

shore to shore.   But why should this be called "London Bridge," when there are so many other London bridges? Because until 1769 the bridge at this point was the only bridge, *the* London bridge; because to-day, in spite of all the rest, it still holds a preëminence as the busiest and most important.   There were once wooden bridges on the Thames, bridges of Roman build, though it seems strange to read of Romans making anything of perishable wood.   Those bridges perished one by one, by fire and by flood. It was about seven hundred years ago that the original stone London Bridge was finished.   It lasted down to 1832, when the structure that we see to-day supplanted it at a point sixty yards above the site of the old bridge of which practically nothing now remains.

Far more conspic-
uous and imposing in
appearance is the new
Tower Bridge which
looks more like a
tower than the Tower
of London, whence it
takes its name. Lon-
don's famous Tower
is undeniably untower-
like and squat. Its
history, however, is
the history of Lon-
don for the last ten
hundred years. Un-
til the time of Queen
Elizabeth it was a
royal residence, and

BYWARD TOWER

for many long years thereafter it remained a prison and a fortress.

IN THE OUTER WARD

THE TRAITORS' GATE

Nothing in London grips the imagination more firmly than the Tower. Who has not shuddered in childhood at the tales told of the London Tower; who has not sorrowed for the boyish princes smothered there, for Lady Jane Grey, Anne Boleyn, Katherine Howard, and the rest who suffered death within its walls; for all the victims of royal hate or jealousy or ignorance who have languished or died within its bloody gates? The Tower, though its aspect has altered with the ages, never has been and is not now a tower, as we understand the word. It is a group of buildings — palaces, prisons, dungeons, churches, chapels, and barracks for the modern garrison — surrounded by strong walls and wide, dry moats. They enclose an area of thirteen acres. The most conspicuous feature is the square pile called the "White Tower," with its four corner turrets. It was built to overawe the city population by William the Conqueror, nearly a thousand years ago. It is not white, but in the year 1240 its inner walls were whitewashed, hence the name "White Tower." The chief sights

A BEEF-EATER

of the Tower are the Crown Jewels and the Royal Regalia, worth fifteen million dollars, the cells of celebrated prisoners, the rooms where Walter Raleigh wrote his "History of the World," the scaffold where the headsman's axe twice made a widower of Henry VIII, the tower where King Henry VI was killed, the tower where minions of Richard III murdered his young nephews —

THE BANK OF ENGLAND

these are among the sights of the Tower of London, the "lions" of the place which every visitor may see as he treads this historic ground under the guidance of a red-clad warder — one of the famous Beef-eaters or Yeomen of the Guard. This well-fed corps is said to derive its name from the old French title "*buffetier*," applied to men who served at the royal buffet in the old Norman days when French was spoken at the English Court; or it may be that they are merely named for what they are, good eaters of good beef, types of Kipling's "four-meal, meat-fed men." They, too, are among the lions of the place, and apropos of the expression

THE GUILDHALL

"to see the lions," we are told that it originated here. There was once a menagerie at the Tower — caged lions were here on view as late as 1834, and it was held the first duty of every visitor to London to see the lions at the Tower; hence the well-known phrase.

London is not one city; it is about thirty towns and villages that have become cities and grown into one another without losing their respective identities.

THE ONLY TREE IN "THE CITY," IN CHEAPSIDE

A TENEMENT

Each is still gov-
erned by its own
mayor and its own
aldermen, each sends its own representative to Parliament, each
has its own town hall, its own business center, its own parks
and pleasure-grounds, and its own parishes.

Of all these united cities, the oldest
and most famous is the one that is
called "The City." It is the
financial and commercial heart
and center of the modern
world, and in the midst of
it stands England's greatest bank — the Bank of
England.

To Londoners there is
a distinction between be-
ing "in the city" and being
"in town." In calling at
the Chelsea home of an English

IN THE EAST END

EAST LONDON

friend, an artist, I asked the servant, "Is your master in the
city?" "No, he is not, sir," he said. "When will he return?"
I asked. "He is here now, sir," he answered. "But you said
he was not in the city!" "He's not, sir; he's at home, here in
the house — he never goes to the City."

IN THE PEOPLE'S
PALACE

Yet there is much that appeals
to an artist in the City: there is the
glorious old Guildhall; and there is
even one real tree, one solitary tree,
growing in Cheapside, famous as the
only tree that has survived the
crowded conditions that have long
prevailed in London's inner "City."

East of the City's acres of
banks and counting
houses, with their
hoarded gold and
never idle talents, stretches
poverty and
that wilderness of
mediocrity called the East End; its misery decently
hid, its horrors screened by the brick walls of its
homes and tenements, outwardly neat in aspect,
reassuring to those who do not look within. But
London is doing much to improve the
housing of her poor. Many model
tenements have been erected by the
London County Council, and there
are many admir-
able institutions, like
the People's Palace in
Mile End Road, where the poor may enjoy all
sorts of necessary luxuries — from books to baths.
But the raising of the "submerged tenth"
must begin with the uplifting of the children.

Childhood is always fair and sweet. The
children of the poor, the respectable poor,
who people the better streets of the
East End, and even the children of
the slums, are for a few brief years

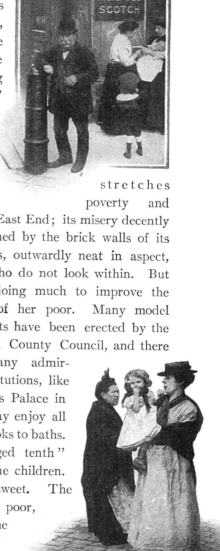

"SEVEN DIALERS"

as dear and lovable and savable as the children of the rich.   Take
any healthy child and wash it clean and it becomes as sweet a
morsel of humanity as any royal baby.   The visitor to the fine
swimming bath of the People's Palace might readily mistake the
youngsters bathing there for the sons of rich or noble fathers;
they are as fair of skin, as full of healthy appetites, and of as
sturdy frame as little dukes or princes;
but they are sons of poverty, and
most of them are doomed to suffer
the vicissitudes of life in the
abyss of the East End.   Their
shoulders soon will bend beneath the burden of their class,
their flesh take on the taint of
East End vices, their minds
be warped by the injustice
of their lot, their lives be
lived in mental and moral
darkness, and their children will inherit a still larger portion of
the curse that artificial civilization has bequeathed to the help-
less poor of the world's overgrown cities.

It is difficult for us to realize the desperate situation of the
empty, unclothed, homeless men and women who people the abyss,
who walk the streets all night because they have no place to go,
and because even the most kind-hearted "bobby" must obey
orders and keep them "moving on."   And on they move.   I have
encountered them at two and three A.M. slouching along, usually
in the middle of   the street, so broken in spirit that they
dared not ask again for the
penny that had been so
often refused.   I have astonished them by offering
a greeting and an un-
expected sixpence, and

"ON THE BENCHES IN THE PARK"

they would look up a little dazed and say, "Oh, good God, guv'ner — thank you!" I have followed them in their aimless wanderings, as they move on from street to street, until at dawn the gates of the great parks are opened, and by some strange dispensation of the powers that be, the men who have been forced to keep awake and *walk* all night past endless rows

PETTICOAT LANE

of East End hovels are freely granted the right to *sleep* all day, stretched on the rain-soaked grass of the aristocratic parks in full view of the palaces of the West End; and there they lie unnoticed by the happy folk who pass by all day long, giving no thought to the so-called drunken tramps, the wrecks of civilization, cast up by the waters of the neighboring abyss.

Living upon the very verge of this abyss, surrounded by it on all sides, yet never falling into it, there is a community of that self-reliant, always self-supporting people, the Jews. Here in East London, as everywhere throughout the world, we find the Jews independent, asking nothing but the right to transact business.

Petticoat Lane is the chief thoroughfare of London's little Palestine.   There
every Sunday morning, while all the
rest of London is wrapped in
Sabbath calm, the Jews
hold their great weekly
market.   We were
given the freedom
of the Lane by the
famous "Kosher

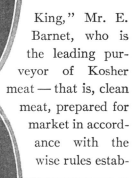

King," Mr. E.
Barnet, who is
the leading pur-
veyor of Kosher
meat — that is, clean
meat, prepared for
market in accord-
ance with the
wise rules estab-

lished by the Jews
in olden times.
Mr. Barnet has
made a goodly for-
tune here in the East
End; some day perhaps
he will be numbered among the very
wealthy Jewish householders in the
fashionable West End.   As George
R. Sims remarked to me one
day, "It sometimes takes the

PEOPLE OF PETTICOAT LANE

Jewish immigrant only
three generations to get
out of Petticoat and
into Park Lane."
This has been done
even in a single gener-
ation. You see the
woman frying fish
there in the window.
Her name is Polly
Nathan, and her
nephew, once a ragged
boy of this Lane, died
as the owner of one of
the grandest mansions
in Park Lane. His
name was Barney

THE "KOSHER KING" IN PETTICOAT LANE

Barnato, the Diamond King of South Africa. Yet Polly Nathan

THE "KOSHER KING" AT HENLEY

A FAMOUS FRIER OF FISH

would not give up her local fame as the frier of the best fried fish in East London, in exchange for all the West End comforts that he offered her.

Toward the wealthy West End we now make our way, pausing to gaze up from the crowded streets at St. Paul's noble dome that seems to float there in the air, high above the throngs that pass through "the Fleet" and across Ludgate Circus and up Ludgate Hill.

The old St. Paul's had perished in the fire of 1666. Some

"BOBBY"

years later, the great architect, Sir Christopher Wren, designed this grander church; he assumed charge of its construction and lived to see it finished in the year 1710. It cost three and a half million dollars, raised chiefly by a tax on coal. The architect received, during the thirty years that he devoted to his task, a salary of

ST. PAUL'S

only about eighteen dollars a week! St. Paul's is the fifth largest church in Christendom. It could be put inside St. Peter's of Rome, and is surpassed in size by the Cathedrals of Milan, Seville, and Florence.

Fleet Street, which is London's "Newspaper Row," ends at Temple Bar, where the famous Strand begins. An inconsequential monument now marks the site of that old archway through which not even Kings or Queens of England could pass in state until they had received the formal sanction of that mighty City potentate, the Lord Mayor of London, who is not mayor of all London, but simply mayor of the "City."

The Bar, built by Wren in 1670, became in time a barrier that impeded the increased circulation of London's most congested artery. It was removed in 1878, when this less obstructive monument was reared. The old stone gate, however, still exists, having been re-ërected at the entrance to a private country seat some fourteen miles   f r o m London; but

here it had stood, a cele- brated land- mark for more than two hundred years, adorned with statues of the Kings Charles I, Charles II, and James I, and from time to time with the heads of criminals on spikes

Close at hand we find the inconspicuous entrance to the famous precincts of the Temple, one of the centers of the legal life of London. These historic courts and

OLD TEMPLE BAR

THE FOUNTAIN COURT OF THE TEMPLE

gardens, through which we may wander in peace and silence from Fleet Street to the Thames, are in the possession of the lawyers' guilds that guard the entrance to the law. It has been well remarked that "there are obvious advantages in having some authority to govern such a profession as the Bar, and it is remarkable that the voluntary societies of Barristers themselves should have managed to engross and preserve it."

A student of law, before he can be called to practice and don the dignity and wig and gown of Barrister, must join one of these old societies, and comply with many antiquated

GOLDSMITH'S GRAVE

LEGAL LIGHTS

usages and customs for the period of several years. But having been called to the Bar by the worthy Benchers, or senior governors of the Inns of Court, he takes up his abode in one of the quaint, quiet corners of his chosen Inn and waits with British patience for his initial brief. The Fountain Court of Middle Temple is one of the calmest and most contemplative corners of all London, a favorite haunt of many old-time Londoners of literary note, like Dr. Johnson, and Charles Lamb; while Goldsmith, another

lover of these Temple shades, still bides not far from here, beneath a simple marble slab on which we read, "Here lies Oliver Goldsmith."

The Temple takes its name from the Knights Templar who one time had their London stronghold here. Their church still stands, and in it lies the effigy of many a

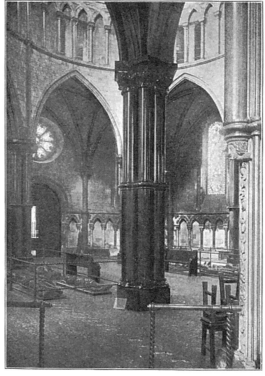

KNIGHTS TEMPLAR

noble Knight, in armor, sleeping his last, his final sleep. Since the twelfth century they have lain here, and meanwhile all their world has passed away. Their mighty order of Militant Crusaders was dissolved in 1313; their Temple then became Crown property.

It is now worth incalculable millions, but for the last few centuries has been leased by the Crown to the legal corporations

THE ROYAL COURTS OF JUSTICE

now occupying it for the amazing sum of ten pounds sterling, or forty-eight dollars and sixty cents a year.

Across the Strand looms the fine modern pile housing the Royal Courts of Justice, and behind it lies Lincoln's Inn, another of those calm enclosures consecrated to the Benchers and the Barristers.

Nathaniel Hawthorne was a lover of those great quiet domains of the various Inns of Court. "Nothing else in London," he wrote, "is so like the effect of a spell as to pass under one of these archways and find yourself transported from the jumble, rush, tumult, uproar, as of an age of weekdays condensed into the present hour, into what seems an eternal Sabbath." Indeed, how much of charm

THE OLD CURIOSITY SHOP

can be lent to an old street or an old house by a graceful paragraph, penned by a man of genius, who can say for us all that we wish that we ourselves had said.

The most potent magic wand is the pen of the great writer; at its touch the ephemeral and commonplace becomes enduring and romantic. Think you that millions of people would have come to stare at a famous little old house near Lincoln's Inn merely because it was old and queer and different from other houses? But the pen of Dickens pointed the way to it, and his world of readers made it a Mecca.

It may, or may not be the Old Curiosity Shop that Dickens peopled with his famous characters — those personages who will continue to live on, in the imagination of his readers. long after all these quaint reminders of the London of his day shall have

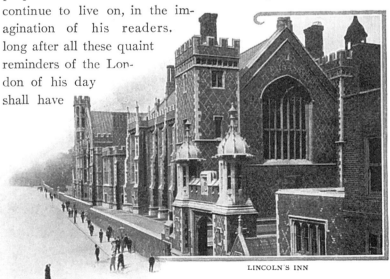

LINCOLN'S INN

ROYAL OPERA, COVENT GARDEN

disappeared — but it has been so long associated with the fame of Dickens that the world resents all doubts as to its authenticity.

World-famous names greet us at every turn in London; and one of the traveler's chief joys is in fitting pictures to these names and then comparing the real picture with his preconception of the scene. The results are interesting, sometimes surprising. "Covent Garden," for example, is not a garden — it stands for both an opera-house and a market-place — yet, it was once the garden of the old monks of Westminster. No vegetables, fruit, or flowers grow to-day there on the site where once industrious holy men raised produce for their monastery tables. The monks are gone, gone is the cloistered garden, but the old name, "Convent Garden" survives, with the loss of one letter, as "Covent Garden," and the sterile pavements witness every morning a colossal trafficking

THE COSTER'S CART

THE GREEN ROOM CLUB

in all the good gifts of nature, from the richest fruits of the far-off tropics to the poorest and prettiest of domestic daisies.

On the stage of the Royal Opera of Covent Garden glitters the same galaxy of stars that shines for us behind the footlights of opera-houses in New York and other cities. The London opera season follows that of New York, beginning in the spring, a happy dispensation for the song-birds of Grand Opera; they need not choose between New York and London; they may twitter merrily in both big cities and add London's guineas to the dollars of New York. Not far from Covent Garden stands another famous

ONE WHO SERVES THE STARS

DRURY LANE

theater, perhaps the most famous play-house of the English-speaking world. It was the scene of the historic triumphs of Garrick, the Kembles, Kean, and Mrs. Siddons, and on its stage Sir Henry Irving made his last metropolitan appearance.

London's theatrical center is at Leicester Square, which may be best surveyed from the windows of the Green Room Club, a club that is to London what The Lambs' is to New York; that is to say, the place where the men whose business is to entertain the metropolis from eight until eleven may, after "business hours," entertain themselves, or find that absolute repose of spirit that can be enjoyed only in company with those who are of *our* kind, or those who, while they may not be "of the profession," know us and *understand*. There stage celebrities are not stared at.

Thus, we can almost pardon the super-exclusiveness of another club — one of London's most aristocratic organizations in Pall Mall — that will not permit even the momentary introduction of a stranger, because, so it is said, each and every member is a personage of such exalted rank or of such world-famed eminence that even the best bred of outsiders would be certain to forget himself and stare at the assembled celebrities in such a way as to disconcert the noble, famous, and self-conscious company.

Leicester Square marks not only the center of theatrical London, but also the frontier of "that foreign country called

LEICE

Soho," where dwells a culinary colony of French, Italian, and Swiss folk, thanks to whose enterprise and skill it is now possible really to dine well and cheaply in London. A marble Shakespeare in the middle of the square gazes reprovingly at two theaters that are devoted chiefly to the ballet. To become *coryphées* at the Alhambra or the Empire is the ambition of all the likely-looking girls of the surrounding quarter. The dancing madness seizes children, maidens, mothers, toddling tots, babies in arms, whenever or wherever a discordant Hurdy Gurdy begins its rapid fire of imported ragtime music. Thus even the poorest "kiddies" of the quarter have their amusements, their music and dancing, their gardens and fountains — all of these things idealized and made delightful to them by the magic of the child's imagination. No doubt their idealized realities bring far more happiness than the realized ideals of grown-up folk, who find in London a satisfaction for every desire, however costly or extravagant.

Armed with this thought, we may approach London's temples of ease, luxury, good cooking, and extravagance,— the ultra-fashion-

ARE

able hotels. The great hotels of London are expensive, and yet not hopelessly so when we compare their charges with those of the greater hotels of the United States. The inner shrine of each of these "temples" is the *salle-à-manger*, at the threshold of which we needs must pause, for during "the season" only the elect may pass its portals, and then only with the consent of the presiding priest in the person of an autocratic and very diplomatic head waiter. The Sunday dinner at the Carlton or the Savoy, when the season is at its height, is a scene not soon to be forgotten; and after dinner, the gorgeously arrayed, sweet-scented multitude masses itself in the palm rooms to discuss coffee, liqueurs, and —

ònе another. These rooms are sometimes so packed with pretty people that the servants cannot circulate. We may weary our eyes with looking at faultless frocks, priceless jewels, and snowy shoulders; but as a rule the men are handsomer than the women.

Another not-to-be-forgotten scene is an after-theater supper at these hotels, when the same dainty, luxury-loving folk arrive — an exquisite array of elegance and beauty — at half-past eleven; a six-course supper is then served as rapidly as possible, for at half-past twelve the restaurant is closed; not closed, as in America, by shutting the outer doors and letting no new-comers in, but closed absolutely, by extinguishing the lights and turning everybody out! And down and out comes all that elegance and beauty to its waiting cabs and carriages and motors. No one protests; Duke and Duchess, financial king and social queen, Lord and Lady, gilded youth and footlight favorite, one and all rise and depart at the polite but firm command of the head waiter. It is as if these people of the ruling class had said to themselves, "We make the laws; we send the working-man home from his public house at half-past twelve, that he may be fit for his work to-morrow; we must observe the rule we make for him; we have not had our salad yet, but

THE SAVOY AND THE CECIL

never mind, *noblesse oblige*, let us go home." How admirable and how un-American!

Un-American, too, is the conspicuous absence of the conspicuous "millinery creations" and "business suits" that spoil the picture in our restaurants. No one may dine or sup or even appear in the coffee-room unless in evening dress. No hats for women and full evening dress for men are the rules, unwritten but rigidly

AT THE CARLTON

enforced. This gives a delightful finish to that attractive show of well-dressed, immensely fashionable, and at the same time immensely well-bred, people. Though there is much animation there is no confusion; though every one is gorgeously arrayed

AT THE SAVOY

no one is conspicuous; though all are talking and laughing the voices and the laughter are not heard — it all resolves itself into a well-bred murmur. They say that the only conversations that rise articulate above the polite hum and buzz of British verbal interchange are the high-pitched conversations of our trans-

Atlantic talkers; the only laughter that rises above the quiet
English modulations is the laughter of the "gent" from "Ar-
kansaw," the "gurl" from "Ioway," or the "folks" of the
newest of New York's new millionaires. And that is why they
don't like us over there in London; they say we have not learned
to modulate the voice. And, seriously, we can't help feeling that
our people are distinctly out of tune with London, that we almost
always talk and laugh hopelessly off their key. This is not to say
that their key is the only well-bred key; in fact, it never seems to
our ears quite sincere, but it is without question a polished key,
and one with which our franker utterance can never harmonize.

THE HOTEL RUSSELL

The tourist center of London is at Trafalgar Square, where England expects every man to do homage to England's greatest sailor, Admiral Lord Nelson, whose form in bronze dominates the square that bears the name of his most famous, and to him fatal, victory. It is difficult to-day to realize all that Trafalgar meant to England. It meant deliverance from the old threat of invasion by Napoleon, for there, off Cape Trafalgar, which is on the coast of Spain, Napoleon's armada of French and Spanish ships was reduced to wreckage by the fire of Lord Nelson's fleet, but there, amid the tumult of his last and greatest battle, the victor died a glorious death! The allies lost nineteen ships out of their thirty-three, but England lost her greatest Admiral, Lord Nelson dying in the hour of victory. The fight was fought October 21st, in the year 1805.

But other features of this great site, frequently called "the finest site in Europe," claim our attention. The perfect Grecian portico of St. Martin's Church is a delight to all lovers of pure classic architecture, and that dumpy, much abused abode of art,

TRAFALGAR SQUARE

the National Gallery, continues to grate on the artistic perceptions of its innumerable detractors.

But oh, the glory of the inner walls of that grimy treasure-house of pictures, containing as it does one of the most important collections of paintings in the world! If it be true, as Hazlitt says, that "a fine gallery of pictures is like a palace of thought,"

THE NATIONAL GALLERY AND ST. MARTIN'S IN THE FIELDS

then does this gallery represent the best thought of all the ages. The best of all is there enshrined; each canvas marks a summit scaled, an alpine height in art, a pinnacle of perfection beyond which human inspiration cannot go. The mere photographer must not profane the temple; let him but pass respectfully before the portico, turn to the left, and halt again before the entrance of another gallery wherein we find the pictured forms of England's kings and queens, her statesmen, warriors, thinkers, and philosophers. It is a national gallery of portraits of the nation's great, from the times of Edward III to those of George V— six hundred years of English history made real for us as we read

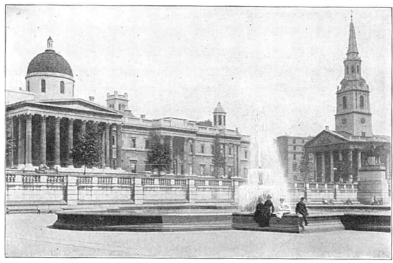

NATIONAL GALLERY AND ST. MARTIN'S

it in the faces of those who played the leading parts in the long, splendid drama of the nation's rise to world supremacy!

In a travel lecture, which must cover so many phases of its subject, there is no room for the contents of London's great galleries and museums. Therefore we may look only at the exterior of the British Museum, one of the richest treasure-houses of the vanished past. The British Museum is not a

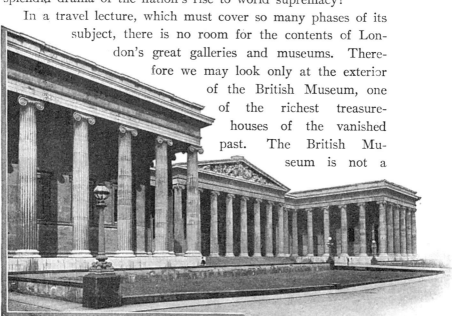

THE BRITISH MUSEUM

mere museum.   It is a *world*, a wonderful world, made up of
fragments of the "world-that-was" before our time.

There in its halls we find the best of antique Greece in the
immortal Elgin Marbles; there Egypt spreads her unwrapped
mysteries before our wondering eyes; there Rome, Assyria, and
all the lands of other days reveal to us, through the medium of
sculptured stone, chiseled metal, or parchments, lettered and

PANORAMA

hieroglyphed, what manner of lands they were, what manner
of life their people led; dead civilizations may be studied there.

But you and I have come to study living London, to see what
manner of life is lived in the London of to-day; and so we come
to Piccadilly Circus to watch the world go by — the commonplace
world of which we are a part, but a world which becomes wonderful the moment that we are content to step aside and for a
space become merely spectators of its every-day doings.

The passings and repassings of the myriad buses, motor-
buses, hansoms, and four-wheelers; the ceaseless crossings and

intercrossings of the human millions is one of the most impressive things in London — one difficult to picture, for in a picture we do not feel the endlessness of the procession.

To get the "feel" of London's streets we should traverse them day after day, viewing them from the outside seats of many buses.

The London bus is one of London's elevating joys; it elevates one from the dead level of the streets, gives one a point of view

CADILLY CIRCUS

that is at once commanding, comfortable, comprehensive, and extremely cheap. The shop-girl on a penny bus may literally look down upon Milady in her smart victoria. But both the buses of the people and the broughams of the swells are indiscriminately halted at every busy intersecting street by the all-powerful and always polite policeman. The hand that wears the glove of the policeman rules the road, and rules it very well. No driver dares to question the silent, firm command of the uplifted hand. The "bobby," as he is affectionately called by a grateful and appreciative public, — the "bobby" is indeed the boss, the autocrat, of the crossing, bringing a semi-silent order and celerity out of what appears about to become inextricable confusion and interminable delay.

The London "bobby" is the Londoner's best friend, the best friend of the stranger. He is found at nearly every corner, a tower of strength and courtesy, feared by the evil-doer, looked up to by

REGENT QUADRANT

the humble, and respected and obeyed by every one. He is an encyclopedia of local information; he answers our questions fully, carefully, and with a fine, respectful civility that is most impressive to us who come fresh from the uncivil cities of our own busy land where no one seems to have time to be polite.

The streets of London do not all teem with traffic. There are long miles of residential quietude, and many acres of park-like peace in the form of little squares adorned with old, old trees, and steeped in a damp stillness that is most refreshing. Fronting on one of these, Manchester Square, stands one of the most notable of London's noble dwellings, Hertford House, to which the world

MODERNIZATION OF THE QUADRANT

is now admitted freely every day. It is the late residence of Sir Richard Wallace, containing the exquisite collection bequeathed in 1897 by his widow to the nation. The contents of this private palace are

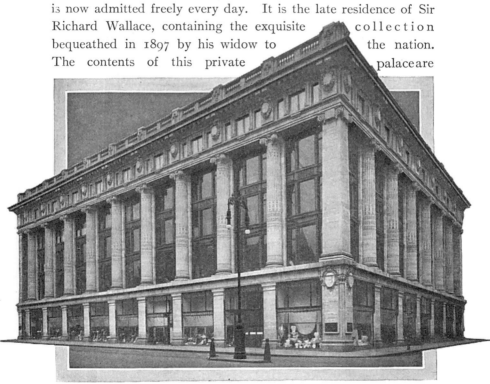

SELFRIDGE'S, THE GREAT AMERICAN DEPARTMENT STORE IN OXFORD STREET

valued at twenty million dollars. The house itself is the "Gaunt House" of Thackeray in "Vanity Fair," and the founder of the collection was the third Marquis of Hertford, who figured in that novel as Lord Steyne. His heir, the fourth Marquis of

QUEEN'S HALL

Hertford, spent his life in Paris, where he indulged in the luxury of buying beautiful things, housing his artistic treasures in that exquisite estate known as "The Bagatelle," that lay, like a mysterious, secluded paradise, in the midst of the Bois de Boulogne, shut in by high walls, and so screened by foliage that its existence was ignored even by many old frequenters of the Bois. The Bagatelle, with its little

A HUMAN SANDWICH

THE MORNING POST, THE WALDORF THEATER AND HOTEL, AND THE GAIETY THEATER

palaces and its spacious park and gardens, has been purchased recently by the City of Paris, and is now open to the public, but the collection was removed to London by Sir Richard Wallace, who had inherited the Hertford millions, lands, and

OUR BILLBOARDS ON THE BUSES

treasures. The late Sir Richard, who rounded out and completed the wonderful collection now known as the Wallace Collection, was a man of exquisite taste and unassuming manner. It is related that one day, resolved to present one of his most valuable

HERTFORD HOUSE

Old Masters to the National Gallery, he himself carried the picture under his arm into the office of the Director, who received him with official frigidity, and was about to reject the proffered parcel and to have his modest visitor shown out, when the latter quietly remarked, "My name is Wallace, Sir Richard Wallace, and I came merely to offer this picture to the National Gallery." The pompous official nearly fainted, for he had been upon the point of rudely refusing that celebrated little canvas by Terburg, called the "Peace of Münster," valued at nearly fifty thousand dollars.

And even when Sir Richard offered to leave his entire collection to the nation, the government raised objections! And when in 1897, seven years after his death, it was finally accepted, experts were sent to examine the collection critically, but although they were instructed to "throw out all the rubbish," they did not find one single object

that could be spared. Not one unworthy object was included in that marvelous collection — each several object represented a masterwork of painter, sculptor, metal-worker, or artistic craftsman of some kind. The array of arms and armor is extremely fine.

Externally, the private palaces of London

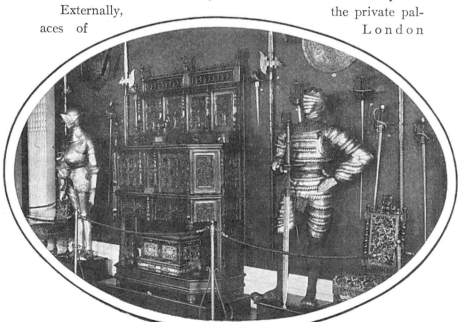

THE WALLACE COLLECTION

are not, as a rule, attractive.   Typical of their grim ugliness is the
side of Devonshire House that fronts on Piccadilly; it looks more
like a dingy old police station than like the dwelling of one of
England's richest peers.   More elegant in outward seeming are the
homes of fashion in Belgrave Square, but the houses of Mayfair, the
smartest of smart neighborhoods, are plain to the verge of ugliness.

Dingy and ugly, too, although imposing in an awkward way,
is that grim and prim old church, St. George's in Hanover Square,
famed for its fashionable marriage ceremonies to the number of

COLLECTED BY SIR RICHARD WALLACE

over a thousand a year — that is, about three weddings every week day! Within St. George's walls many of our fairest and richest daughters of democracy have been joined in holy wedlock to scions of old English families, or to the sons of our own millionaires; for it has become quite the thing for our wandering wealthy to be married far from home, and the fashionable fame of St. George's in Hanover Square appeals to them with all the force of recognized tradition. Another famous building in this same quarter is Burlington House, home of the Royal Academy and scene of the great exhibitions of modern art. The annual exhibitions are undeniably great in number and variety of canvases, although much of the art there represented falls far short of greatness, and we are amazed to find on the walls of so famous a gallery so many pictures that would be unworthy of a place even in an art student's show in a minor American city. But in criticising British art and London architecture, the American must not overlook the thousand and one things which are done better in England than

DEVONSHIRE HOUSE

in America. The London "lifts," or elevators, for example, may be crude and slow, but the "lift attendant" is *polite*. The buses may be antiquated, but the bus conductor still collects the fares with old-time courtesy; such insolence and rough handling as are meted out to passengers in our own up-to-date subways and trolley cars would not be tolerated for a moment by the citizens of London.

BELGRAVE SQUARE

It cannot be denied that there is a finish and refinement about things English that many things American, despite their material superiority, most sadly lack. To employ a very far-fetched illustration, yet one that will at once make clear just what I mean, glance at the fac-simile, on page 59, of a bill for services that was presented to me by a London dentist. I had asked for my account. I received by post what I at first mistook for an engraved invitation to a ball or a banquet. I sent a check for the amount; a few days later came another exquisite specimen of engraved stationery, acknowledging the receipt of my prompt but paltry payment, and with it a portrait of his Majesty, King Edward, for no receipt

is legal unless a penny stamp has been affixed and duly cancelled.
Contrast this with what we should expect at home — a printed
bill-head, with these words writ thereunder:

"To filling one cavity, $15.00

Please remit,"

and the subsequent brusque and abbreviated

"Rec'd paym't.

Dr. James

Per Rosie Driggs, Stenog."

Of course we say that we have not time for all that "polite non-
sense," but isn't it agreeable just the same?

Park Lane is the upper Fifth Avenue of London.   To engrave
the words "Park Lane" upon a calling card is almost to transform

THE RITZ

that card into a social passport. The mansions of the Park Lane millionaires overlook Hyde Park. For the most part they are less splendid externally than the American palaces that front on Central Park. Of the interiors I saw but one — that of the town house of Lord Brassey, who kindly gave me the freedom of the private museum, filled with the artistic spoil of many of those famous voyages made by the late Lady Brassey in her yacht, the "Sunbeam." A more delightful museum I have never seen. Every object treasured there recalls or represents some interesting experience or some rare acquisition in some far corner of the world. Lord and Lady Brassey have been everywhere, and always in their own yacht, on which, by the way, my old guide in Morocco, Haj

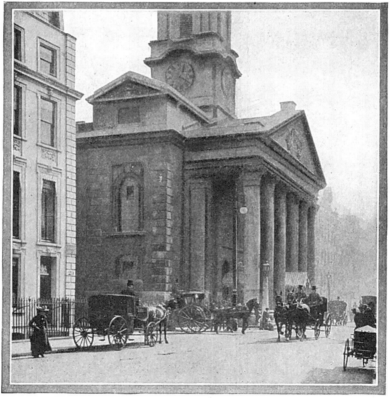

ST. GEORGE'S IN HANOVER SQUARE

A BILL AND A RECEIPT

Abd-er-Rhaman Salama, once served a long apprenticeship as cook; and as we viewed the treasures there in that Park Lane mansion we recalled the tone of triumph with which Haj Abd-er-Rhaman used to announce to us, as we pitched our camp in all the discomfort of a rainy night on the desolate Moorish plain, "Never mind, gentlemen, to-night I make you a dinner like I used to make for Lady Brassey on the 'Sunbeam.'"

To appreciate the elegance of the West End, the traveler should come to Hyde Park Corner directly from the East End — so near and yet so far away. Orient and Occident, England and Asia, are not farther, one from another, than the poverty-stricken East End of London from the splendid West End of the world's richest city. As we gaze at the pillared portico of Apsley House, given by England to the Duke of Wellington, the stately front of Rothschild's residential palace, the dignified façades of other rich men's dwellings, the noble abodes of fashion in Belgravia, the spacious streets,

the flowery balconies that overlook the shady squares — all these
things speak of wealth and luxury, of the very refinement of
elegance, the commonplaceness of extravagance. London is
indeed the best city in the world for the rich; the worst for the
poor. In Whitechapel, families of seven working and starving

PARK LANE

in one room with the rent collector at the door. In Mayfair,
seven idle ladies drinking seven dainty cups of tea, with seven
idle footmen waiting at the door. In Mayfair the very thought
of poverty becomes absurd; life seems one everlasting holiday and luxury, the normal lot of man. But doubtless there
are many homes in Mayfair where the slaves of fashion find it
difficult to make the two ends meet. However, the West End as a
whole is wealthy; the entire Empire pays it tribute. It owns the
crowded tenements of the East End; it owns rich lands in England
and in Ireland; its capital has been invested in the surest and most

profitable enterprises in all corners of the world. We feel behind this great perpetual display of wealth, of which Hyde Park is the chief scene and center, the toiling millions of two hemispheres, the peasants who are tilling other people's lands, the workers who are doing other people's work, the clerks and employés and managers of vast concerns throughout the world, who are helping to earn the dividends for the shareholders here "at home."

The splendid expanse of Hyde Park — six hundred and thirty acres of park land in the heart of residential London — was once church property known as the Manor of Hyde. Henry VIII made it a royal park; Queen Elizabeth's subjects hunted deer in Hyde Park; those of Charles II came to see horse races here; those of King Edward come here to be seen and to see one another's clothes — especially on Sunday, at the hour of the weekly "Church Parade." Hundreds of women beautifully gowned, hundreds of men in the traditional frock coat and silk hat of the English gentleman, come to Hyde Park after church, not necessarily *from* the churches, but after church time, and then for an hour or more fashionable London stares at itself in these

DORCHESTER HOUSE; RESIDENCE OF THE LATE AMBASSADOR REID

perfumed pathways that skirt the "little paradise that's called
Park Lane." On weekday afternoons crowds of humbler folk
assemble to watch the fashionable driving in "The Ring." No
cabs or buses, carts or wagons are allowed to circulate within
the park; the splendid show of rank and fashion is not marred,
as is the case in the Bois de Boulogne of Paris, by the presence
of public cabs with broken-down horses, unkempt drivers and
cargoes of cheap, ill-dressed people who, in coming to see the
pretty people, spoil what would be, without such intruders, a
most artistic show. In Hyde Park the smart set and the plain
people do not try to mingle. While wealth and elegance go
driving round the Ring and over the bridge across to the Serpentine, the plain folk go rowing up and down that noble sheet
of water, showing their plebeian shirt-sleeves and having a much
better time than the fine folk in their carriages.

The Serpentine is an artificial lake, but seen from the bridge it
presents a vista which has, as Henry James has said, "an extra-

HOMES OF WELLINGTON AND ROTHSCHILD

ordinary nobleness"; at least Baedeker says that Henry James said
that, and we, looking upon the noble view, agree that Henry James
has spoken well.   Not quite so apt was the remark of the American who, as he watched the wretched oarsmanship of the cockney
crews trying to row their little boats along the Serpentine, ex-
claimed, "So that's why they call it Rotten Row!"

Of course he was mistaken.   Rotten Row, as every one should
know,   is a long, wide bridle-path taking its

THE GATEWAY AT HYDE PARK CORNER

name from the old French name of the old "Road of the King,"
the "*Route du Roi.*"   You see how relentlessly the English
Anglicize their old French names.   Think of it — *Route du Roi*
turned into Rotten Row!

That English men and women are devoted to the horse becomes
at once self-evident to any one who watches the equestrian parade
in Rotten Row.   Some of them carry their devotion to their dogs
even beyond the grave.   The little dog cemetery in Hyde Park,
near Victoria Gate, is to some people the most interesting Campo
Santo in all London.   There lie the deceased pets of aristocratic

families. These pets were chiefly canine, a few feline, several avian and two or three simian — but most were just dear dogs. Let me read a few epitaphs that I copied at random: "Jack, a faithful friend"; "Here lies Sappho, far from my eyes, near to my heart"; "A perfect dog, Plato"; "Schneider, aged 18"; "Jack the Dandy, a sportsman and a pal." Then there are three

IN HYDE PARK

tombstones near together bearing the names of three dogs who in life were utter strangers, but whose names are now inseparably linked in the memory of every thirsty visitor,—"Scottie," "Paddie," and "Whiskey." Upon another stone I read, "A little Dog with a Big Heart."

London has twelve great parks, and forty-nine great squares that are practically parks, to say nothing of the open stretches of country, such as Hampstead Heath and Epping Forest, reserved as playgrounds for the London poor. Hyde Park and its adjacent green spots, St. James's and Green Park and Kensington Gardens are the most precious possessions of the denizens of the great city. Surrounded on all sides by the abodes of wealth, these parks form almost a continuous green carpet, here and there overspread with gorgeous floral rugs. One summer Sunday I went forth to enjoy a day with Nature. I tramped or loitered on all day, covering not less than ten good miles, yet never going beyond the limits of these parks, and scarcely coming within sight of the encircling streets. I simply wandered round about St. James Park, skirting the pretty lakelet, or following the winding walks amid the shrubbery. I zigzagged across the open meadows of Green Park, struck out across the prairies and lost myself in the little forests of Hyde Park, finding it difficult to believe that all this lay in the heart of the great city. Yet it is a splendid fact that London has embraced and will preserve so long as London lives these fragments of the fragrant, living country, these acres of God-made reality and beauty, in the midst of her countless square miles of man-made artificiality and ugliness. Many charming little bits of beauty are discovered by one who gives a day to a diligent exploration of these royal parks, around which crowds a population of of over seven millions. The wonder is that the parks are not packed with people all the time — that there is room for all this quietude and calm. It is strange indeed when we think of the pressure of the dense multitude without that this

THE "CHURCH PARADE"

great vacuum, this area of land unoccupied and empty, should not
be filled instantly to overflowing by an irresistible inrush of humanity from the congested regions round about. This happens
only now and then, as the result of some slight socialistic agita-
tion of that encircling human sea. Wave after wave of decently

THE SERPENTINE

dressed and earnest men rolls quietly in from the surrounding
streets, settles into a calm sea of faces upturned toward the orator,
who is thundering a condemnation of the existing order of things.
I sat throughout an afternoon among the speakers on the wagon
used as a rostrum.   I listened in amazement to the most outspoken
abuse of the government, yet not a protest came from any of the
many bobbies within earshot. The working-men listen attentively,
applaud with discrimination, and when the show is over pick up
their gorgeous banners and march off as they came, in orderly,

well-ordered ranks, obeying every behest of the polite but firm policemen. Apropos of the gaudy insignia of the various Trades Unions seen on such an occasion, we observed with satisfaction the picture on the banner of the Amalgamated Society of Tailors. It represented Adam and Eve in the Garden of Eden, thus

ROTTEN ROW

quietly reminding us that man owes a great deal to his tailors! Some men owe more than others, but they don't use banners to advertise the fact.

The turf of these great parks is remarkably fine. We recall the English gardener's recipe for turf, "Take two hundred years," and the little school-girl's definition of turf, "Turf is grass and clean dirt put together by God"; but how all that perfect turf and all the pretty flowers and all the grand old trees in the parks and club domains in London can continue to exist is indeed a mystery. We suppose that smoke and soot are fatal to plant life, and we know, or rather we are told by scientific observers, that on every square mile of London's area there are deposited one thousand two hundred and forty-eight tons of soot every year; in other words, every square mile of this closely built metropolis is receiving a coating of solid matter, precipitated by the smoky fog at the rate of about three

and a half tons a day! Yet English trees OF THE PRIVILEGED CLASS and grass and flowers keep on growing in this province of brick that is called London. But how urgent and important it is that the remaining green and open spaces in and near London should be kept green and open and as blessedly wild and uncultivated as possible. And this is being done. If the rich have their Country Clubs at Ranelagh and Hurlingham on the southwest, the poor have their Epping Forest rolling away in wooded loveliness on the northeast, and they have Hampstead Heath lifting its bare,

breezy hills on the northwest. "Breezy,"
however, is not the word for 'appy
'ampstead on a 'oliday; "cyclonic"
or "tempestuous" better defines
the conditions that prevail there
on Bank Holiday. For a definition of Bank Holiday I must
refer you to the composition of
an East End school-boy who
wrote, "They call this happy day

Bank Holiday, becos the banks
shut up shop so as people can't
put their money in but has to
spend it. Bank Holidays is the
happiest days of your life, becos
you can do nearly what you like
and the perlice don't take no
notice of you."

THE CANINE CAMPO SANTO AT
VICTORIA GATE

It is on a Bank Holiday that one sees the Cockney in his element. What is a Cockney? No Londoner will admit that a Cockney is a typical Londoner, yet all the world regards London as a community of Cockneys. Why is that epithet, Cockney, universally applied to a man who lives and dies in London. One good authority assures us that it is derived from an old expression,

THE COACHING CLUBS MEET

"a cockered child," meaning an effeminate fellow, a derisive appellation for a townsman in contrast to the hardier peasant or countryman. Another explanation of the origin of the word is more amusing. It is related that in olden days a city father took his city son for the first time into the rural districts. A horse out in the fields gave utterance to a sound strange to the ears of the astonished city lad. "Father, what does the animal?" he asked. "Son, the horse neighs," replied the well-informed wise parent. "But, father," said the boy a moment later, as he heard for the first time a rooster's voice, "Father, does the cock neigh, too?" And so they called the little Londoner a "Cockney." This is probably from "Punch."

There is of course a distinction between the Cockney and the Coster. The real Coster is a peddler, and he owes his name to an apple. Long years ago the peddlers most popular and prosperous were those who sold a special kind of apple called a "Costard

IN ALL KINDS OF WEATHER

Apple." As they sold Costards they were called Costard-mongers. Then the "d" was dropped and they became Coster-mongers, and to-day, although they have branched out from the apple trade and are engaged in peddling many kinds of food — from fruit to garden truck — they owe their title "Coster" to the apple that brought fame and some share of fortune to the peddlers of the past. At least this was the story as told me by a Londoner who knows his London very well — no less an authority than Mr. George R. Sims, who has written much of the "Living London" of recent years, and who from week to week comments cleverly on

TALLY HO!

the doings of the London of the passing moment in his celebrated column, "Mustard and Cress," in one of the most popular weeklies of the metropolis. One day I had the pleasure of showing Mr. Sims something in his own London he had never chanced to see — to take him to one of the few restaurants which he had never visited — the American Quick Lunch in the Strand. He gazed in wonder at the peculiar paraphernalia that are essential to the attainment of trans-Atlantic speed in serving food; he watched a few New Yorkers bolting their mid-

AROUND THE RING

RANELAGH

day meal.   When I asked him what he would like for luncheon, he replied, "Just a streak of lightning with electric sauce!" "The lightning has just struck," the imported waiter said, so Mr. Sims partook of corned-beef hash, hot cakes, and, what to a Londoner is the deadliest of all American mixed drinks — made of ice and water.   As I have not had the pleasure of his company since then, I begin to fear that I have sacrificed the respect and confidence of that eminent native upon the altar of an alien cuisine. London of   course has its own   kind

HURLINGHAM

of quick lunch, too, — admirable restaurants where wholesome food is served with celerity at very modest prices.   Amusing to the American are many of the little economies practiced in the cheaper establishments; for example, if you wish to save a penny, simply do not ask for a napkin; if you do insist upon one, an extra charge of two cents will appear on your check.   But even

CRYSTAL PALACE

in the most modest places you will find the courtesy that is so sadly lacking in American cafés of the corresponding class.   When you give your order, the waitress will say "Thank you" — but she says it so quickly that it sounds as if she had merely interrupted a silent saying over of the alphabet, to pronounce aloud the letter "Q."   Again, when you accept the proffered roll, she murmurs "Q"; when you complain that the beef is too well done, a polite "Q" is all you hear; the same short sound of "Q" or "kew" is evoked by the bestowal of your two-cent tip; and as you take your hat to go, she "kews" an adieu and you "Q" the gods that you are to escape at last from her monosyllabic gratitude.

There are times when the American is tempted to cry out against the too insistent courtesy of the servants in the restaurants and hotels, or of those who serve in the shops. It all seems to argue both a lack of self-respect and an appalling absence of any sense of humor. There is a servile, subservient, cringing, and, strangely enough, at the same time contemptuous mien, peculiar

IN CRYSTAL PALACE

to the salesman or saleswoman in the fashionable shops, that amazes and offends the shopper from "the States." I encountered one day a peculiarly aggravated case of humorless humility and self-satisfied *hauteur*. It was in one of those *recherché* art galleries in Bond Street — the daintiest and most expensive shopping street in London. I had dropped in to look at an exhibition of water-colors there exposed for sale, but — one of the littlenesses of London — the prospective purchaser had to pay a shilling for the privilege of looking at the pictures, with which the shopkeeper hoped to win his custom. The young man in charge, clad in a long frock coat, escorted me formally from frame to frame, rubbing

his hands softly together and murmuring unctuous responses
and indorsing very humbly any criticism I might make. "Yes,
Sir, quite so, Sir — indeed, Sir — you are quite right, Sir — oh
yes, Sir, very true, Sir"— until I wanted to seize him by the beard
and smite him into some semblance of self-respect. He seemed
to respect me so much that I resented it, and when he made his
one bold stroke and spoke right out and said, "May I ask, Sir —
may I take the liberty of inquiring, Sir — of what class of pictures
does *your* collection consist" — I could not resist assuring him in
an equally earnest tone, "My collection consists merely of all
the great canvases by all the great masters, of all the famous
schools" — and as he looked   blankly at me, I added, "and
for convenience I keep them   in such places as the National
Gallery, the Louvre, the Pitti   Palace, and the Vatican, and I
travel around from   time to time to
look at them,"   whereupon

THE ALBERT MEMORIAL

he murmured, "Oh, indeed, Sir," but without any trace of impolite astonishment in his well-modulated voice. Probably to himself he said, "Another of those mad Americans!" All that servility may perhaps be taken seriously by the English gentleman as a matter of course, but to the American, accustomed to the free and easy address of the I'm-just-as-good-as-you-are employé, it is as exasperating as is to the Englishman the seeming rudeness of our

"AMERICA"

people. Englishmen delight to tell of how they have rebuked what they regard as the unpardonable insolence of the lower classes in America. One very clever British actor, who has toured the States several times, has one unfailing method for humbling the haughty personage who collects tickets on the trains. When the free-born, independent, and usually disdainful conductor, without so much as "if you please" or "by your leave" taps him on the shoulder, thrusts a hand in his face and gruffly growls "ticket! ticket!! you!!!" the injured Thespian looks up, adjusts his monocle, and in a very earnest, pleading tone replies, "I know, my deah Mr. Conductor, that in foah short yeahs you may become President of these United States, but please don't be unkind to *me*."

Nor is rudeness unknown in courteous old England. Let the well-dressed man risk himself in Battersea Park or on the Heath on one of those Bank Holidays, and he will find that London's merry-making multitudes have little real respect for anything or anybody unless it be the bobby.

Another popular resort for London's multitudes is at Sydenham, eight miles from London, where the famous Crystal Palace

THE ALBERT HALL

looms grandly, like a colossal bubble curiously shaped. The great glass house is more than sixteen hundred feet in length, and its nave one hundred and seventy-five feet high. The glass and iron that enter into its construction were first used in the building of the first great Industrial Exposition held in Hyde Park in 1851. This Crystal Palace commemorates the opening of the epoch of those colossal industrial shows that we now call World's Fairs.

Crystal Palace is in a sense a permanent World's Fair, offering us in its beautiful Courts of Art and History splendid retrospective glimpses back along the past of many civilizations, and offering, at the same time, in its galleries and concert halls much that is new and beautiful in art and music, while in its gardens and arenas we may witness from time to time thrilling spectacles of strong appeal to all sorts and conditions of men — foot-ball battles fought in view of cheering multitudes; ballets danced on lawns under the light of the summer moon by sweet children clad in classic garb; glorious pyrotechnic miracles that blaze against the blackness of the night; or assemblages that thrill us as we were thrilled one day at sight of sixty thousand Salvation Army soldiers, from nearly every nation of the civilized world, passing in review before their grand old chief, great General William Booth, who, with his "beak like a scimitar of conquest and his beard like a banner of victory," stood there in all the glory of his seventy-five years of youthful enthusiasm, an inspiring picture, the latest and one of the greatest of the Prophets — a Prophet who himself, by his own efforts, brought many of his noble prophecies to pass.

In Kensington Gardens near the site of that Exposition of 1851, of which the Crystal Palace is the conspicuous memorial, rises that marvelously ornate thing of questionable beauty, the Albert

FOR THIRTEEN THOUSAND AUDITORS

Memorial, erected, as the inscription tells us, by "Queen Victoria and her people to the memory of Albert, Prince Consort, as a tribute of their gratitude for a life devoted to the public good."

At the four corners of the terrace stand four sculptured groups, each representing one of the four quarters of the globe.

KENSINGTON PALACE AND STATUE OF QUEEN VICTORIA BY HER DAUGHTER, PRINCESS LOUISE

VICTORIA AS A CHILD

Every American will survey with pride the marble allegory of "America." Fronting the monument looms that most imposing of the world's auditoriums, the Royal Albert Hall, a modern Colosseum devoted to the divinest of all earthly arts — the art of music. It has echoed to all manner of melody from the voice of Patti to the rousing hymns and thundering drums of the Salvation Army. The Hall has seats for an audience of nine thousand, but it is possible, using the spaces for standing spectators, to crowd thirteen thousand persons into the Albert Hall.

Not far from these memorials of the good Prince Albert, who died in 1861, stands the palace that was the girlhood home of Queen Victoria, who will always be thought of as "Victoria the Good." She was born in Kensington Palace in the year 1819, on the 24th of May. In the same palace she learned of the death of her uncle, King William IV, in 1837, and hither came those who

QUEEN VICTORIA AND HER IMPERIAL AND ROYAL RELATIVES IN 1897

ALEXANDRA

were charged to announce to her, a girl of eighteen, that she was to be crowned as England's Queen and Empress of Great Britain.

The story of her reign of over threescore years is the story of the Golden Age of England.

It was Victoria the Good who first made Buckingham Palace the official Royal Residence in London. Before her time it had been occupied only occasionally by George III. George IV gave it its present form in 1825, but never lodged within its somber walls. In style it might be described as "respectable," an eminently sober, dignified, and unappealing piece of architecture — a fit abode for personages of the highest principles and direst lack of esthetic sensibilities. Well might the English Queen remark to the Duchess of

Royal Portraits by
W. and D. Downey, London.

EDWARD VII

QUEEN MARY AND KING GEORGE V

Sutherland, her hostess, at Stafford House, the finest private house in London, "I have come, Duchess, from my *house* to your palace!"

In plain English, Buckingham Palace is an ugly building, lacking even the medieval quaintness that redeems the dingier ugliness of the little old-time Palace of St. James, where Victoria's royal predecessors

THREE GENERATIONS

had held their Court ever since the days of Good King Hal, who reared its "dumpy" walls of brick and its "dinky" crenelated towers nearly four hundred years ago.

The American, thrilled by accounts of the splendors of the "Court of St. James's," cannot believe his eyes or ears when he first beholds that insignificant, rambling pile of dirt-colored brick

BUCKINGHAM PALACE

and is told that it was the home of royalty for many generations. It stands where a leper hospital founded in 1190 had reared its even uglier walls for three and a half centuries, and something of the repellant horror of that vanished pile seems to still cling to the old site despite the glamour given it by centuries of royal pomp and dignity.

Formerly the great royal functions — the "Drawing Rooms" and the "Levées"— were held at St. James's. Now Buckingham Palace is the scene of the gorgeous "Drawing Room" ceremonies where ladies are presented to the sovereigns; but the "Levées," at which only gentlemen are presented, are still held in the older

palace, waking into life, from time to time that grim little royal
residence which still gives its name to the Court of England's
King. Foreign powers still accredit their Ambassadors and Min-
isters to "The Court of St. James's."

But the traveler sees not the inner richness of these royal
palaces; the mere "man in the street" must be content with
glimpses of the royal carriages as they come and go, and with the
brief daily spectacles presented at the moment of the changing
of the guard. Every day, or nearly every day, we may see a
company of the Scots Guards—or the Coldstream or the Grena-
diers,—preceded by a splendid band, come swinging into the
old Friary Court to perform the snappy, almost automatic cere-
mony of relieving guard.

Another pretty little military show may be witnessed every
morning just across St. James's Park in the Court of the Horse

IN STAFFORD HOUSE. THE TOWN HOUSE OF THE DUKE OF SUTHERLAND

Guards which fronts upon Whitehall. There waits a troop of the King's Life Guard. Just on the stroke of eleven a bugle sounds, and through the archway sweeps another little troop of the finest looking soldiers in the world. The secret of effective uniform belongs to Britain's army; even the long rain-coats worn by the men about to be relieved are as effective in their way as are the polished cuirasses of the plumed knights who have just come upon the scene. As for the men themselves, they are magnificent; each one a perfect specimen of British dignity and brawn. Their horses, too, are model mounts, and in all the world there is no prettier military sight than that presented by a passing troop of his Majesty's Life Guardsmen.

Once every year, on the birthday of Queen Victoria, May 24, a splendid scene is witnessed on the Horse Guards' Parade. It is called "Trooping the Color," and on that occasion the military display is magnificent and satisfying. The space is comparatively small, the massing of the redcoats wonderfully effective — far more so than it would be on a larger field.

THE GUARD AT ST. JAMES'S PALACE

Dominating that crowded Field of Mars, gory with the blood-red uniforms of Britain's defenders, looms the huge building where the wars are made, for it houses the Foreign Office, the Home, the Colonial, and the India Offices. It fronts on Downing Street, that plexus of the nervous system of the Empire. Here, in Down-

THE HORSE GUARDS

ing Street, dwells the Prime Minister, and in these palaces of Downing Street the policy of England is determined. Downing Street is the brain of Britain, and the decisions of Downing Street, acted upon by Britain's fleets and armies, become the deeds that are in time writ large upon the page of history.

Many new Government buildings have risen in and near Whitehall; among them the new Admiralty, the new War Office, the new Government Office, new Scotland Yard; yet all these modern piles possess that British faculty of looking old and thoroughly "in the picture," harmonizing with — or at least not marring — the mellow, age-worn aspect of this marvelous old city which is modernizing itself without making itself *new*.

Therein lies the charm of London — in this happy harmonizing of the old and the new. But London's charm is slow in taking hold upon the stranger. It is more subtle than the charm of other cities. Paris, for example, makes instantaneous appeal to the affections of the "Man from Other-

RELIEVING GUARD

where." The newcomer instantly feels at home in Paris, loves Paris at first sight. To see Paris is to love Paris: but to love London one must know London.

Though to the newcomer a city seemingly inhospitable, London becomes in time, to a greater or less degree, according to the worthiness and merit of its guest, a place of such delightful and interesting experiences that a sojourn there must ever remain a gracious and ennobling memory. There is no other city in the world that offers so much old-time charm, combined with so much that is best in modern life — old London, dreaming calmly, undisturbed by modern London's roar — new London, with its pulsing enterprise, guided, controlled and made delightfully livable by the spirit of the old.

It would be a wonderful experience to explore London under the guidance of one who knows the ins and outs of London life, the queer old nooks and corners, the novel little sights that the casual sight-seer never sees. Such a guide would show you where the first cup of coffee ever made in London was brewed, tasted and consumed. That was in 1657, when a barber by the name of Farr, whose shop was in Fleet Street, got himself in trouble with his neighbors by concocting a strange new hot beverage from a bean imported from the Orient; in fact he was sued by the parish for "making and selling a drink called coffee, whereby in making the same he annoyeth his neighbors by evil smells." That was more than two hundred and fifty years ago. I cannot answer for the smells to-day, but I do know that London coffee still annoyeth by its evil taste.

Another sight our knowing guide would surely show us would be the ancient vestige of a Roman bath, in a little street just off the Strand. How many of us even suspect that there is a Roman bath in London? There are unsuspected sights to be seen at every turn in this wonderful old city which was once upon a time

LIFE GUARDSMEN

a Roman camp. How many of us have ever made our way through the damp darkness of the Adelphi Arches from the roaring Strand down to the broad, beautiful embankment? Yet every time we go along the Strand from the Savoy or the Cecil to Trafalgar Square we pass the entrance to that tunnel-like thoroughfare,

"TROOPING THE COLOR"

which is even to-day grimly suggestive of the dark deeds that made it notorious in the old days when the favorite rendezvous of thugs and criminals was in those vaulted passageways that lie beneath the Adelphi Terrace.

"TOMMIES"

Then there is a new subterranean London, the labyrinthine under-London of the tubes and of the modernized electrified old Underground Railway, the tunnels of which have been clarified of the smoke and gases that for so many years threatened every passenger with asphyxiation. American example and enterprise have transformed the old underground transportation system, and

THE FOREIGN OFFICE

endowed London with many miles of new transportation tubes, through which Londoners are shot in electric trains that move with satisfying celerity, though not with the amazing speed and long runs of the expresses in the subway of New York. There are practically no surface lines of electric cars in the heart of London. Suburban trolley lines have their city termini on the edge of the congested inner districts; here the old horse-bus, though threatened by the motor-bus, is still supreme. There may be "no buses running from the Bank to Mandalay," but there are buses from the bank to every part of London — and again I urge the stranger within the gates to stick to the top seats of the old bus as the best point of view from which to study London town. The taxicab of

course has come to stay; the once popular and always leisurely
hansom cab is doomed, and it's a hard blow to that large class of
worthy men, the hansom drivers, who have for years served London faithfully. Most of them are too old, with too much *horse*
sense, ever to learn how to drive a gasoline car. The average
Londoner is not adaptable — "once a cabby, always a cabby,"

DOWNING STREET

applies just as truly as "once a gentleman, always a gentleman."
But the gentleman now hails a taxi and the cabby is left with his
antiquated two-wheeled relic of the motor-less age, standing idle
on the "rank." Although London increases in area from year
to year, it does not seem one half as big as it did in the old slow-
going days; the automobile seems to cause a town to shrink and to
become compact; it brings the distant parts near to one another
and alters the atmosphere of each by robbing it of its remoteness.

One of the latest additions to London's list of noble buildings
is the new Catholic Cathedral which lifts its tower — called St.
Edward's Tower — nearly sixty feet higher than the twin towers
of Westminster Abbey, which may be seen as we look eastward

from its top.   In style, the new Cathedral is early Christian Byzantine, rich in effect and yet not costly, for the material is plain red brick and simple stone.   The interior, however, when completed, will be rich and gorgeous beyond anything outside of Italy.   The nave, higher and wider than any nave in England, will blaze with beautiful mosaics, the chapels will be gems of the mosaic makers' art, rivaling those of Ravenna, Venice, and Palermo. The Catholic Cathedral of Westminster will take its place as one of the foremost sights in this the foremost city of all Christendom.

THE CATHOLIC CATHEDRAL OF LONDON

It is fitting that the tower of the newest great house of Christian worship in London should bear the name of "Edward,"— Saint Edward the Confessor, — the Catholic Saxon King who built the greatest and most famous of the churches of old London, Westminster Abbey. The Abbey site has been a holy one since the year 616, when an earlier Saxon monarch, King Sebert,

TOWARD WESTMINSTER FROM ST. EDWARD'S TOWER

erected there a little church in honor of Saint Peter. Even to-day, the Abbey is officially known as "the Collegiate Church of Saint Peter." Its more familiar name, Westminster Abbey, it owes to the old Benedictine Monastery, or Minster, called Westminster to distinguish it from the now vanished Cistercian Abbey, called Eastminster, which stood near the Tower of London, on the site now covered by the buildings of the Royal Mint. To the left of the Abbey, as we face it, stands the little church of Saint Margaret, containing the tomb of Walter Raleigh, who was executed just behind the church in 1618, and the tomb of William Caxton, the pioneer of printers, who worked his famous printing-press in an old almonry that stood where now we see the Westminster Column, a monument to the heroes of the Crimean War and the Indian Mutiny. The west front of the Abbey is not beautiful; the graceless towers added by Sir Christopher Wren, early in the eighteenth century, spoiled the beauty of the Early English edifice; but the interior of the nave has not been marred, and it is now as overwhelmingly impressive, in these modern days of George V, as it was in the medieval days of Edward I, under whom the building assumed the magnificent proportions and satisfying beauty that make it still the grandest temple in the world's metropolis. Fortunately, we may enjoy the glorious vista of the nave without having our eyes offended by the awful so-called "works of art"—the monu-

THE TOWERS OF WESTMINSTER

ments — that have filled the side aisles and transepts of the Abbey as with a fearful sculptural nightmare.

Those marble monuments that England has reared in honor of her great dead there in Westminster Abbey are painful testimonies of the bad taste of the generation which stood sponsor

WESTMINSTER ABBEY

for them. It is a pity that there could not have been a censorship of monuments as well as a censorship of plays. Plays, if bad, will perish of their own demerits; but marble monuments, however atrocious, endure for generations.

But the names of the great men of whom those marble eyesores are the memorials will be remembered as long as history endures. Even to give a list of those great names would fill too many pages. Heroes and poets, statesmen and soldiers, — men who "filled history with their deeds and earth with their renown,"

lie here beneath the marble pavements of the Abbey; and on the
tablets, columns, or mortuary monuments that mark their resting-
places we read such famous names as Gladstone, Darwin, Newton,
Herschel, Pitt, and Kingsley; such beloved names as Garrick,
Thackeray, Dickens, Spenser, Browning, Tennyson, Matthew
Arnold, and Sir Henry Irving; and although not interred in
the Abbey, Shakespeare, the poet of all ages and of all men, and

THE NAVE OF WESTMINSTER ABBEY

THE CHOIR OF WESTMINSTER ABBEY

KING HENRY'S CHAPEL

our own Longfellow have their places marked there in the Poets'
Corner, where, as Addison says, there are "many poets who have
no monuments and many monuments which have no poets."

But there in the Abbey sleep not only those who achieved
greatness, but also those who were born great or had greatness
thrust upon them.   The Abbey is the sepulcher not only of those
who reigned by right of the royal gifts of mind and intellect and

IN WESTMINSTER ABBEY

genius, but also of dead Royalty, of those who were doomed to a certain sort of greatness from their birth. For most of them greatness meant either great misery or great misfortune. The chapel of Edward the Confessor is literally "paved with princes."

The lesser chapels that surround it are peopled by a host of noble folk whose titles recall page after page of England's history;

THE HOUSES OF PARLIAMENT

and in the greater chapel — Henry VII's Chapel — that is a distinct and separate structure, and yet forms a part of the great church itself, lies a company of royal dead whose names evoke visions of the great glories and the greater tragedies that have marked the historic turning-points in the life-story of the English-speaking race.

Henry VII, who died about four hundred years ago, was an artist and a builder of consummate taste. He sleeps to-day beside his Queen, beneath the most marvelous stone roof ever devised by man. It has indeed "the airy security of a cobweb"; there indeed we see stone "robbed of its weight and density" by the patient chisel of the artist. Beneath that same exquisite canopy sleeps a silent royal company, united in death, though in life no bonds, save bonds of hate or bonds of interest, existed between Queen and Queen, or King and Prince, or Monarch and Protector. Here lie Mary, Queen of Scots, and Queen Elizabeth. Here lie the little Princes who were smothered in the Tower by order of their uncle, Richard III. Here lie William and Mary, Queen Anne, George II, the last King buried in the Abbey, and the sixth King Edward, who sat on England's throne from 1547 until 1553 as the successor of Henry VIII, and who was like him a champion of the Reformed faith. Here lies, also, King Charles II, and here was buried for a time the mighty Lord Protector of the Commonwealth; but Oliver Cromwell's bones were dragged forth after the Restoration and cast into a pit at Tyburn, and his head, the head that ruled England well, the head that had been deemed by the nation wiser and better than many of the heads that had worn the English crown,—that head of Oliver Cromwell was fixed loosely on a spike and suspended on one of the pinnacles of old Westminster Hall not fifty yards distant from this chapel of King Henry, where for a time Oliver Crom-

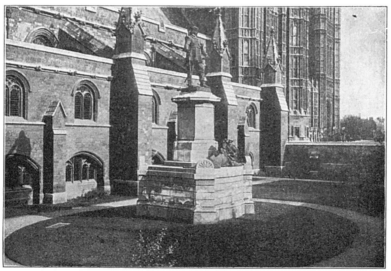

OLIVER CROMWELL

well's body lay in company with the dead monarchs of his land.
For over thirty years that skull of Oliver Cromwell, rattling on its
spike, was exposed to the gibes and execration of his enemies,
until at last a kindly, blustering wind blew down that skull; a
sentry picked it up, sold it, and so it came, in time, into the possession of the descendants of England's uncrowned king.

To-day a statue of the Lord Protector stands near the spot
where men once gathered to gaze up at the head of Cromwell

THE NEW PALACE OF WESTMINSTER

as it hung there on the turret, an eloquent reminder of the fickle-
ness of fate,—doubly fickle when we recall the fact that it was
in Westminster Hall that Charles I, Cromwell's predecessor,
was condemned to death, and in it Cromwell himself was invested
with the sovereign power. Westminster Hall is the oldest portion of the vast group of buildings called the Houses of Parliament. The Hall itself dates back nearly a thousand years,
while the greater part of the huge adjacent pile, officially
known as the New Palace of Westminster, is modern.

In fact it dates from 1841 and replaces a building burned in
1834. The architect was Sir Charles Barry, whose design was

chosen as the most beautiful and practical among the ninety-seven designs submitted in the competition.

The area covered by the structure is no less than eight acres; there are eleven courts; there are one hundred stairways; there are eleven hundred rooms! The material, unwisely chosen, is a stone called Dolomite. Nature herself has given the world a

THE HOUSE OF PEERS

conspicuous object lesson, proving that Dolomite is not an endur-ing stone: the picturesqueness of those famous mountains in Austria — the Dolomites — is due to its susceptibility to weather-ing. Just as the Dolomite peaks and pinnacles are crumbling and weathering away under the influence of the winds and rains, the heat and frost of the Tyrol, so the graceful pinnacles, turrets and towers of this range of architectural Dolomites, in London, are suffering and losing their perfection of outline and detail under the influence of the winds and rains, the heat and frost of the

harsher British climate.   As yet no really appreciable damage
has been done, but a beginning has been made: a century
hence England will have striking proof that a less friable material
should have been chosen for the palace of her Parliament.

The two great towers of the Houses of Parliament are among
the most graceful towers of the world.   Perfect in its feminine

THE HOUSE OF COMMONS

grace and dignity is St. Stephen's Tower, whence comes the
frequent booming of "Big Ben," the best-loved bell of London;
perfect in its masculine grace and majesty is Victoria Tower,
rising above the royal portal through which the Sovereign enters
when he comes to open or to prorogue Parliament.

To indicate that Parliament is sitting, a Union flag flies from
Victoria Tower by day or a light gleams from St. Stephen's
Tower by night, and ofttimes the light gleams steadily the whole
night through.   All night and all day, every quarter hour — the

thirteen-ton bell in that clock tower tells the time to listening London, and London listens gladly to "Big Ben" whose gentle boom can penetrate the thickest fog, reach waking ears on the far outskirts of the town and yet not trouble those who sleep even within the shadow of the tower.

Big Ben is called big because it is big, and Ben because the First Commissioner of Works, under whose direction the big bell was hung, was Sir Benjamin Hall, whose memory is kept resonant by the booming bell that bears his name. How much more effective, as a memorial, is bronze in the form of a living, speaking bell, than bronze in the more artistic, but voiceless form of a statue or a tablet. The bell reaches the ears of millions every hour; the monument catches the eye of only a few score in a day. Great men should pray that bronze bells instead of bronze effigies should be cast to commemorate their lives and deeds.

The British Parliament has been called the "Mother of Parliaments." It sat as one house until the reign of Edward III when the Knights and Burgesses began to sit apart from the

WESTMINSTER BRIDGE

Peers. This was the beginning of the House of Commons, which has since then exercised and guarded very jealously the taxing function. Originally the right to sit in the older House came not through noble birth but through land tenure: the Parliament was simply a council of Feudatories. It now con-

THE PEOPLE'S FORUM IN TRAFALGAR SQUARE

sists of about six hundred members including twenty-eight Dukes, — owners of vast estates — thirty-six Marquises and two hundred and eleven Earls. The oldest Dukedom is that of Norfolk, established in 1483, the newest, that of Fife, dating only from 1889. The earliest

Marquisate is that of Winchester, the newest, that of Linlithgow. The Earl of Shrewsbury's title goes back to 1442, the Earldom of Liverpool is as modern as the "Lusitania," dating from 1905.

These Peers sit in the grandiose chamber of the House of Lords to discuss, year after year, the weighty questions that concern the nation's welfare, superbly unmindful of any expressions of the nation's will.   The world waited patiently from year to year for what was to have been the crowning culmination of the labors of the Peers, the answer to the burning question, "May a man legally marry his deceased wife's sister?"

This question has at last been answered in the affirmative, but only after generations of debate and serio-comic bitterness. And now the Peers have flung the gauntlet down, refusing to recognize the to them appalling fact that the Feudal Age has passed away; that the world has kept on moving even since their predecessors, the great nobles of seven hundred years ago, forced King John to sign the Magna Charta at Runnymede in the year 1215. Each Peer now finds himself in King John's ancient shoes, or, to

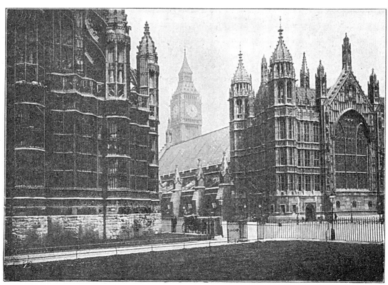

A GLIMPSE OF ST. STEPHEN'S TOWER

be accurate, in the sandals of that thirteenth century King, who in the face of the armed protests of his Lords and Barons, yielded, just as the Peers themselves, in the face of the protests of the People, must in the end yield also. It should be now King and People arrayed against Ancient Privilege. The Sovereigns of England's mighty Empire must stand, if they would stand at all, with the People, for they are no

longer the auto-crats, the law-givers, as were the Kings of old.

THE TOWERS AND TURRETS OF THE LORDS AND COMMONS

The Sovereigns of England rule by the grace of Tradition and through the love and respect of their loyal subjects, — subjects as free, as independent, as the citizens of any Republic in the world to-day. The House of Peers may dally with dead issues, may delay the triumph of democratic principles; the Sovereigns may wear their crowns, lay corner-stones, bestow decorations, and play the leading parts in social life and do devotedly their endless tasks of public charity, — all this is well and nobly done by England's King and Queen, but the real Sovereignty of England, as of the United States, rests with the People; and it is in the House of

Commons, not in the House of Peers, that we hear the voice of the Nation — giving commands that Kings and Peers and Commons must obey: there a free people speaks its will through its representatives in Parliament assembled; there the most gifted sons of a great race are laboring conscientiously for the wise conserving of the Old that is good, and for the diligent upbuilding of the New that must be better if the greatest Empire that the world has ever known is to hold its preëminence among the nations of the future.

FURTHER READING

W. W. Norton published *The Complete Book of London* (1992), and the commentary contains excellent historical information about the city. For additional insights, see also G.R. Elton's *The English* (1992). An engrossing 30-minute videocassette, *London,* covering London's several diverse sections is distributed by International Video Network (1994).

Anyone who wishes to find out about the major events and personalities of Europe between 1875 and 1914 should read Eric Hobsbawn's *The Age of Empire: 1875-1914* (1989). Other inter-esting books on the period include *Europe 1815-1914* by Gordon Craig; James Joll's *Europe Since 1870;* and *A Survey of Euro-pean Civilization* (Vol. II, from 1660), by Wallace K. Ferguson and Geoffrey Brown. See also: Barbara Tuchman, *The Proud Tower* (1966); Edward R. Tannenbaum, *1900: The Generation Before the Great War* (1976); and *War by Timetable: How the First World War Began* (1969), *The Struggle for Mastery in Europe, 1848-1918* (1971), and *The Last of Old Europe: A Grand Tour* (1976), by A. J. P. Taylor.

—Dr. Fred L. Israel

CONTRIBUTORS

General Editor FRED L. ISRAEL is an award-winning historian. He received the Scribe's Award from the American Bar Association for his work on the Chelsea House series *The Justices of the United States Supreme Court.* A specialist in American history, he was general editor for Chelsea's *1897 Sears Roebuck Catalog.* Dr. Israel has also worked in association with Arthur M. Schlesinger, jr. on many projects, including *The History of U.S. Presidential Elections* and *The History of U.S. Political Parties.* He is senior consulting editor on the Chelsea House series *Looking into the Past: People, Places, and Customs,* which examines past traditions, customs, and cultures of various nations.

Senior Consulting Editor ARTHUR M. SCHLESINGER, JR. is the preeminent American historian of our time. He won the Pulitzer Prize for his book *The Age of Jackson* (1945), and again for *A Thousand Days* (1965). This chronicle of the Kennedy Administration also won a National Book Award. He has written many other books, including a multi-volume series, *The Age of Roosevelt.* Professor Schlesinger is the Albert Schweitzer Professor of Humanities at the City University of New York, and has been involved in several other Chelsea House projects, including the *American Statesmen* series of biographies on the most prominent figures of early American history.

IRVING WALLACE (1916-1990), whose essay on Burton Holmes is reprinted in the forward to The World 100 Years Ago, is one of the most widely read authors in the world. His books have sold over 200 million copies, and his best-sellers include *The Chapman Report, The Prize, The Man, The Word, The Second Lady,* and *The Miracle.*

INDEX